CUTHBERT COLLINGWOOD
The Northumbrian Who Saved the Nation

Andrew Griffin

First published in October 2004 by
Mouth of the Tyne Publications
Reprint April 2005
5 Bruntley Meadows, Alston,
Cumbria. CA9 3UX
andy@griffin5199.freeserve.co.uk
www.cuthbertcollingwood.co.uk

Cover picture courtesy of The Society of Antiquaries of Newcastle upon Tyne

Dedicated to great grandfather, David Griffin, keelman, born 1740s and a neighbour of Cuthbert Collingwood.

ISBN 0-9548698-0-X

Printed by Robson Print Ltd.
Haugh Lane Industrial Estate
Hexham, Northumberland
NE46 3PU

CONTENTS

'Now, gentlemen, let us do something today which the world may talk of hereafter.'

Rear-Admiral Collingwood, 21st October 1805, Trafalgar.

ACKNOWLEDGEMENTS

Family: Pat, sons Oliver and Barnaby and brother Gordon
Rebecca Griffin, Kamila Zamaro and Jordi Ballart
Charles 'Brian Aldridge' Collingwood
David and Mary Phillipson for their invaluable genealogical research
Michael Morris, David Middleton, Craig Turnbull and John Vinton
Janice Irving, Joan Bower, Peter Charlton and Elaine Pope at BRIC, Blyth
The Blyth Readers
Blyth Library, Newcastle Central Library and Record Office
Eric Hollerton at North Tyneside Central Library
Alastair Robertson, Johan Rossouw
Members of the Literary and Scientific Society of Blyth
Tynemouth Watch House
Friends of St Paul's Cathedral, London
Maritime Museum, Greenwich, London
Portsmouth Historic Dockyard
Hartlepool Marina - especially staff on HMS *Trincomalee*

ABOUT THE WRITER

Andrew Griffin was born in Newcastle in 1944 and has spent most of his life within a pebble's throw of the River Tyne. Andrew, a teacher by trade but writer and historian by inclination, has written many plays and books with a regional theme. His formative years were spent in Whitley Bay during the town's heady days as a seaside resort and he remembers Tynemouth long sands and Collingwood's monument as a favourite childhood haunt. It was years later, when Andrew, as a North Tyneside guide, became aware that very few people knew about the life and times of Cuthbert Collingwood. The book is intended to revive the memory of a forgotten hero. Andrew, and wife Pat, have recently moved from Tynemouth to Alston in Cumbria - from the mouth to the source of the Tyne.

FOREWORD

October 21st 2005 marks the second centenary of the Royal Navy's victory at the Battle of Trafalgar over the combined forces of the French and Spanish fleets. Great Britain will once again, deservedly, celebrate Admiral Lord Nelson's heroic contribution. Defeat would undoubtedly have led to the invasion of our island nation, Napoleon's superior land army would probably have forced the British into subjugation and I certainly would not have been writing this 'Foreword'.

Nelson, however, did not achieve the success on his own. The Norfolk admiral was mortally wounded at an early stage in the conflict and he was removed from the scene, leaving his second in command, Rear-Admiral Cuthbert Collingwood, to oversee the battle and receive the swords of surrender from his country's enemies.

For Collingwood, the campaign did not end on the 21st October. The ageing seaman, who had spent barely four years on English soil since joining the navy at the age of twelve, was obliged to stay in foreign waters to keep the peace and ensure that Britannia ruled the waves. For the following five years he controlled the British fleet in the Mediterranean and he was destined never to return to his beloved wife and daughters.

Cuthbert Collingwood was modest, brave and wise but it was his devotion to King and Country and his unwavering sense of duty that set him apart. After Trafalgar he continued the unglamorous task of patrolling the seas and blockading the ports. His constant vigilance allowed Britain to arm itself for the showdown at Waterloo when Napoleon Bonaparte was finally defeated.

As a distant relative of the Northumberland family I have known of Lord Collingwood's achievements and I feel honoured to share the family name. I am also aware that there has been no recent publication that adequately tells the story of the great Vice-Admiral... until now. Andrew Griffin's research is thorough and the fascinating events of Collingwood's life and death are described in persuasive and compelling detail. The people of Tyneside may be surprised to learn of the influence that Cuthbert Collingwood exerted during the Georgian period and the impact he had on world events. This entertaining book celebrates, and reaffirms, the place in history of one of the North East's greatest sons.

Charles Collingwood
Brian Aldridge of The Archers BBC Radio 4.

TRAFALGAR
The Prelude

Heart of oak are our ships, heart of oak are our men: [1].

It was noon on the 19th October 1805 when Lord Nelson began writing to Lady Emma Hamilton. He told his mistress:

> 'The signal has been made that the enemy's combined fleet are coming out of port. We have very little wind, so that I have no hope of seeing them before tomorrow.'

Nelson's second-in-command, Vice-Admiral Cuthbert Collingwood had been keeping a close watch on the entrance of Cadiz, in the Straits of Gibraltar, and he had seen the gathering of the French and Spanish fleets over the past few months, and now, after weeks of watching and waiting, the enemy were leaving their safe haven to face the Royal Navy in combat. The warning flags of the British frigates nearest the port were raised so that the information could be passed back from ship to ship to reach Nelson, the Commander-in-Chief, who was out of sight, beyond the horizon, some fifty miles away.

Twenty-four hours later, Nelson added a paragraph to his letter and explained to Emma the strength of the combined forces of the enemy:

> 'They have committed as far as forty sails of ships of war, which I suppose will be thirty-four of the line and six frigates... May God Almighty give us success over these fellows, and enable us to get a peace...'

The letter remained unfinished and these would be the last words he would write to his beloved Lady Hamilton. She would receive them after his death.

At the time of writing, the winds were light, and they would remain that way for the next twenty-four hours. It was not unusual for the warships to take hours to prepare for the battle formation. It was a difficult task to communicate to the widespread fleet and even more difficult to manoeuvre the ships into their fighting positions of attack and defence in an unpredictable sea.

Collingwood was situated where he could see the formation of the enemy and he described their line as 'a crescent, convexing to leeward'. France and Spain were well prepared to defend themselves against the British onslaught. They knew what sort of attack to expect and they had placed a double line of ships which were curved like jaws to snap at their enemy.

Lord Nelson

Horatio Nelson had been appointed as Commander-in-Chief by King George and the Prime Minister, William Pitt (the younger) a month earlier and he joined the fleet on September 27th. He took over the command from Collingwood and arrived without the usual ceremony, as he did not want the customary fanfare and gun salute to alert the enemy. Nelson was much feared and respected by the opposition and it was conceivable that if they knew of the Admiral's arrival, then they might remain securely in port and not venture out.

The French commander of the fleet was Admiral Pierre Villeneuve and his Spanish counterpart was Admiral Gravina. The two men were allies but they did not see eye to eye. The Frenchman was pressurised by Napoleon Bonaparte, who expected the navy to be as successful at sea as his military forces were on dry land. Villeneuve was anxious to satisfy his leader and he held a council of war on October 7th in which he declared that an early strike at the British was essential. The Spanish held a different view. Gravina believed that his own new recruits were not ready for battle as they were untrained and inexperienced. There was also a grudging acknowledgment of their enemy's supremacy. He confessed to the French Admiral:

'The British have kept the seas without intermission since 1793, while most of our fleet have scarcely weighed anchor for eight years. Only a madman would think of sailing in the present circumstance. Do you not see Sir, that the barometer is falling.'

The Spaniard implied that there was a change in opinion against a headlong battle. It was reported that Villeneuve replied with a sneer, saying:

'It is not the glass, but the courage of certain persons that is falling.'

Gravina was deeply offended by the remark and by questioning his bravery and honour, Villeneuve was almost drawn into a duel as his Spanish ally threatened him across the table. When order was finally restored, it was agreed that an attack would take place if conditions proved favourable.

In spite of Villeneuve's apparent lack of tact, he was highly regarded by the British seamen, but not it seems, by Napoleon Bonaparte. The recently crowned Emperor of France was becoming impatient and he was having

Admiral Villeneuve

serious doubts about Villeneuve's abilities. His irritation with his naval commander led him to persuade Admiral Rosily to come out of retirement and take over the fleet. Rosily agreed and set off overland to take control. Villeneuve was well aware that his authority was in question and whilst he waited to be relieved of command, he received the news that the British had sent two of its men-o'-war vessels to Gibraltar for fresh supplies of water. The French leader welcomed this information and convinced himself that Nelson's decision to remove the ships from his fleet (leaving only twenty-seven ships-of-the-line) would be enough to fatally weaken the British. Villeneuve decided that this reduction would tip the balance in favour of the combined force and he visualised a glorious overwhelming victory. His command outnumbered the Royal Navy and he was safe in the knowledge that he had more fire power in his mighty ships. The terrifying *Santissima Trinidada* was the largest fighting ship in the world with 130 guns on board and next came the Santa Anna with well over a 100 cannon and each ship had a crew in excess of 1,000 men. The men of the Royal Navy felt an awesome respect for these ships but they were not feared, in fact the reverse was true; such was the confidence of the British seamen, that they relished the opportunity of taking on the enemy's strongest vessels. They were very keen to show their foes that Britannia really did rule the waves.

Collingwood and Nelson were very close friends and they were both in agreement that this forthcoming battle was crucial to the survival of Britain. Napoleon Bonaparte was intent on crossing the channel with his Grand Army to overrun the island, just as that other Frenchman, William the Conqueror, had done almost 750 years earlier. There was no question that Napoleon had the armed forces to take England. He had overwhelmed the European landscape, and beyond. The Emperor demanded, and expected, the same dominance of the sea. He had actually drawn up a plan for his navy, ten months before Trafalgar, in which he confidently expected to plot the downfall of Nelson. Napoleon issued instructions to his admirals and he expected them to be carried out with military precision - he refused to accept that sea conditions were unstable and not as predictable as dry land. Villeneuve, against his better judgement, had obeyed his leader's orders and sailed the French fleet out of Toulon in January 1805. He managed to evade the blockade set up by Nelson's squadron and he headed, as instructed, directly for the West Indies. On the way he was to meet up with the Spanish fleet and ships from Northern France and together they would sail back to Europe with an invincible armada. Bonaparte expected Nelson to pursue the French fleet to the West Indies, which he did, and they anticipated leaving him behind whilst they got on with the business of invading England. It did not work out as the Emperor had planned - many ships missed the Caribbean rendezvous and it was an inexperienced depleted armada that returned to Europe in a bedraggled, sprawling convoy. Nelson was disappointed to have missed an encounter with the enemy but his superior seamanship brought his squadron quickly back to European waters almost at the same time as Villeneuve. No advantage had been gained by either side and although the French did have the opportunity to practice sailing on the open sea the exercise had ended in stalemate. The blockading continued as before.

It was a very frustrating time for Napoleon Bonaparte, for he had his 115,000 soldiers camped at Boulogne, trained and ready, at a minute's notice, to board the specially designed landing crafts that would take them onto the British beaches. The French had already made two incursions into Wales, and although unsuccessful, they were serious attempts at a landing - invasion was not an idle threat. The Admiralty publicly ridiculed the attempts of their Gallic enemy and

Lord Jarvis, tongue-in-cheek, said that Napoleon had the force to invade, but if they did, it would not be by sea. So how else could they cross the channel? The satirical cartoonists made a great play of showing a small, fat Napoleon Bonaparte looking enviously towards England whilst above him there are decorative balloons, drifting out of control, with anxious troops hanging from their suspended baskets. This was a topical reference to the French Montgolfier brothers who had demonstrated manned-flight and flown for a distance of six miles in their hot-air invention.

A cartoonist's satire on the balloon invasion

It had been several months since the West Indian debacle and now, on the morning of the 21st October 1805, the enemy formed their defensive curve and waited whilst the two divisions of the British fleet sailed inexorably towards them. It was a beautiful day as the cloudless sky reflected its vivid blue onto the Atlantic Ocean; an unlikely setting for the bloodiest sea-battle in the history of naval warfare. At mid-morning, in the lightest of breezes, the Royal Navy was sailing its warships at little more than walking pace into the teeth of one and a half thousand loaded cannons. Cuthbert Collingwood was leading the division that would attack the rear and Nelson would head directly for the front, or van, of the enemy line. Nelson's second-in-command, in the *Royal Sovereign*, was the first to make contact with the waiting French and Spanish fleet and he bravely drove his ship into their line, in spite of the tremendous fire he came under. It would be an hour before the battle got under way and already the Northumbrian Admiral was at full sail and prepared to take on the enemy without support. Nelson watched the actions of his close friend and could only admire his determination. He declared:

'See how that noble fellow, Collingwood, takes his ship into action. How I envy him!'

At the same time Collingwood said to his captain:

'What would Nelson give to be here!'

From the *Victory*, Pasco the signalman, was keeping his eye trained on the *Royal Sovereign* and he reported:

'There is a top gallant yard gone!'

Nelson was anxious:

'Is it the *Royal Sovereign*?'
Pasco reassured him:
'No, my Lord, it is the enemy.'
Horatio was delighted:
'Collingwood is indeed doing well.'
His friend continued to do extremely well for the next eight hours until darkness fell. During this period Nelson would forfeit his life and Collingwood would assume command and lead the fleet to victory; a success that saved the nation from invasion and the tyrannical rule of a foreign power.

The Royal Sovereign leading the attack on the enemy rear.

CUTHBERT COLLINGWOOD
Cabin Boy to Lieutenant

Come cheer up my lads! 'tis to glory we steer.

Cuthbert Collingwood was born at The Side in Newcastle upon Tyne on the 29th September 1748. The quayside street still overlooks the River Tyne and it was here that young Cuthbert spent his formative years. The Collingwoods lived in an imposing residence surrounded on all sides by tightly-packed insanitary streets and dark squalid housing. This bustling, seafaring location left a deep impression on the future admiral and it is said that as a youngster he would often make the short voyage across the river from Newcastle to Heworth aboard his father's keels. The sturdy, powerful keelmen, in their distinctive blue bonnets, ruled the river in the mid 18th century as they rowed their deep boats, laden with coal, to the large vessels at the mouth of the Tyne. For most collier ships, the meandering River Tyne was too shallow and dangerous for the journey upstream to the city of Newcastle and the waiting coals. The ship owners were dependent on the hundreds of keels that delivered the 'black diamonds' to their vessels from the riverside landing stages. The keelmen would shovel out their coal into the colliers' holds, level it off, then return to collect another load. The constant traffic of these rough and ready sailors, just beyond young Cuthbert's front door, was a backdrop to his first twelve years.

The Collingwood family were descended from a long illustrious Northumberland line who had established themselves in Eslington on the banks of the River Aln, forty miles north of Newcastle. Their land was in the English Middle March district in the late 16th Century when the border reivers, or thieves, were at their most violent and

The Side 1850

The Side 2004

lawless. The reivers would steal cattle and crops, and attack peaceful homesteads, murdering the inhabitants and setting fire to their farms. In the 1580s Sir Cuthbert Collingwood became a high-ranking border official and courageously stood up to the Scottish and English raiders. One of the most feared gangs at that time was the Burns' clan and they embraced some of the country's most notorious criminals. One dark evening these marauding thugs decided to target Sir Cuthbert's neighbours and they successfully rounded up a large herd of cattle and drove them towards the Scottish border. When the alarm was sounded, the robbers were pursued in what was known as a 'hot trod' or posse. Thieves who were overtaken could expect no mercy and blood was often spilled, hence the expression 'caught red-handed.' Jock Burn knew of the consequences for rustling and in the melee that followed, Collingwood killed him, legally. On hearing of his brother's death, Geordie Burn exacted cruel revenge and invaded Collingwood's estate and murdered seventeen of his people (a contemporary account claims the fatalities numbered thirty-five). Burn was later caught and hanged but Collingwood had barely recovered from the attack when he was besieged yet again in the winter of 1587. This time it was the ruthless outlaw, Robert Kerr. Kerr had brought a band of 2000 men from Scotland into Collingwood's territory and a group of raiders were sent to attack Sir Cuthbert's home. He, his two sons and six servants came out of the house and bravely took on the robbers in a hand-to-hand fight before being driven back indoors. Eventually the English infantry arrived and pursued the attackers. Sir Cuthbert joined in and 'followed the fray.' In the event 150 prisoners were captured and all but thirty head of Collingwood's cattle were recovered. The Northumbrian knight endorsed his warden's intention, when he stated:

'By the time I have hanged 40 or 50 of the prisoners, which I will do at the least, I trust they shall have small cause to boast of that journey into England.'

The Christian name 'Cuthbert' was passed on through the family's first-born sons until it reached the future admiral. Clearly his ancestor's bravery and willingness to fight against the odds when facing the enemy, was a genetic transference 150 years down the line. Young Collingwood's father was also named Cuthbert but unlike his son, he lacked the famous family drive and determination. Collingwood senior was an unsuccessful businessman and although he traded on the quayside, it was the wealthier branch of the family that propped him up. It would be left to his three sons to revive the dwindling family fortunes.

Cuthbert's father married his mother, Milcah Dobson of Appleby, and they had ten children - the first seven being girls. Of the seven, only three girls survived into their youth, but after reaching their teens, Mary lived to be 77, Dorothy 89 and Elizabeth 95. None of the daughters married for there were no dowries on offer and no financial inducements to attract a husband. Their father saw the girls as a drain on the family resources. It was an overcrowded family home and living in such close proximity with his sisters, inevitably young

Cuthbert got to know them well. Judging by the care and concern expressed in the letters that he wrote home in later life, he clearly felt a deep affection and obligation towards his sisters. When his father died, he took over the responsibility for their security and well being.

Cuthbert was the eighth child and heir and in spite of seven earlier attempts to produce a male offspring, Milcah now gave birth to Wilfred and John to complete a trio of brothers. Wilfred would also have a successful, if short-lived, naval career and he would sail with Nelson and Cuthbert in the Caribbean. John was destined to stay firmly on shore where he became a high-ranking customs official. John would outlast them all and live to see his 90th birthday – astonishing longevity for the Georgian era.

Cuthbert Collingwood senior died in 1775 in his sixty-third year. This was the year that his eldest son, now aged twenty-seven, was promoted to the rank of lieutenant. It was an important step-up as it meant Cuthbert junior (or now senior) would be an officer on the quarterdeck and would qualify for substantial prize money in the time of war. The lieutenant became the head of the household and he was aware that it was his duty to provide for his mother and sisters at home. On 15th September 1783, at the age of thirty-five, he wrote to his eldest sister:

> 'Whenever it is in my power to contribute to your ease and comfort you
> must trust that I will. I have no pleasure in my successes, but as they enable
> me to assist those who need my help. My pleasure is to administer the
> means of happiness to you my sisters, and I will most willingly do whatever
> is in my power towards it. There is peace now and no prospect of prize
> money.'

America had signed a treaty at Versailles and Britain was for the time being 'in amity' with Spain and France so there would be tranquil times ahead. There was no possibility of a financial bonus to supplement the relatively poor pay that Collingwood would claim on completion of his voyage. As a lieutenant he received a monthly salary of £5.12.0d [five pounds twelve shillings = £5.60p] and only half of that sum was paid if the officers were ashore on 'stand by' in peacetime. The Admiralty made war an attractive option and the promise of accommodation, food, adventure and glory, helped draw in many able-bodied volunteers. The Royal Navy's man-of-war ships were floating killing machines so they became redundant and laid up when peace broke out.

The lack of income for the Collingwood family should not have arisen, for although their father was unable to provide for his wife and children without help from relatives, it was actually young Cuthbert's grandfather who had brought them to near-penury. Later in life, as Vice-Admiral of the Fleet, Collingwood would describe how his grandfather had neglected the affairs of the family 33 years before his birth. It seemed that his descendent George Collingwood of Eslington had taken part in the 1715 rebellion that attempted to regain the English throne for the Scottish Stuarts. Great Uncle George was a close friend and supporter of the Earl of Derwentwater, a leader of the Jacobite uprising, but sadly his choice of ally was ill judged. George Collingwood was rounded up and hanged at Liverpool and his estates were forfeited to the crown; the money raised from their sale helped pay for Greenwich Hospital in London – ironically Cuthbert's penultimate resting place on his final journey to St Paul's Cathedral in London. Grandfather Collingwood, the heir, unlike his wayward brother, had always supported the Royalists and it was said that 'on proper application to the King' his loyalty would have been rewarded and the estates would have stayed in the family. The Collingwood neighbours, the Forsters of Bamburgh, were in the same predicament and after a royal appeal their lands were restored to them. Had his grandfather petitioned King George, the young seafarer would probably have grown up in rural Northumberland, miles from the coast. He would have inherited the estates and farmed the land under the shadow of the Cheviot Hills. Cuthbert Collingwood became such a vital commander in the Royal Navy, that it seems inconceivable that the nation could have managed without his leadership. In spite of the pull of the sea, there was still a place in Cuthbert's heart for his native Northumbria even though he spent very little time at home during his lifetime. It has been suggested that Collingwood would have risen up the ranks quicker if he had settled in the influential South of England but he chose to set up his family home in Morpeth, over three hundred miles from the nation's capital. When he was offered a peerage after Trafalgar he chose to return to his roots to become Baron Collingwood of Caldburne and Hethpool after his properties in College Valley near the Cheviot foothills.

Collingwood's parents may not have been wealthy but they did insist that their sons attend the local Royal Grammar School, which by chance, had as their headmaster the Rev Mr Hugh Moises – one of the most forward thinking educationalists of his day. The Newcastle RGS records reveal that boys entered the school at the age of eight and were educated up to the age of sixteen or seventeen. In the late 1700s the school was situated on the opposite side of the street where Newcastle's imposing Central Station now stands today. Collingwood would arrive at school for a 7am start and would finish his studies at 6pm although he was allowed a two-hour lunch break. His route was up the

The first Royal Grammar School in the late 1700s

The old RGS gatepost still visible in 2004

steep and narrow Side to reach St Nicholas's Cathedral and from there it was a short level stretch to the school entrance. Young Cuthbert would walk to and from his school twice daily, six days a week, for several years. On his journey the eight-year-old would never have imagined that sixty years later, the area would become part of Richard Grainger's ambitious city development, and that this very route he plodded upon, would be named Collingwood Street in his honour. The Royal Grammar School was moved to the suburbs of Jesmond where today it still enjoys a reputation for its high standard of academic attainment.

Cuthbert was only there for four years but the influence of the Reverend Moises would have been deeply entrenched. Before 1750 the Newcastle school was not in the front rank of educational establishments but that was to change. Under the inspirational headmaster, its reputation grew and parents from a wide area, who sought a career for their sons, were happy to enrol their boys. In the 18th Century there was very little distinction between tradesmen and the professions, both serve an apprenticeship before becoming fully pledged members, and even though the RGS curriculum was principally based on classical studies, it nevertheless provided the pupils with a broad learning foundation.

Many pupils left the school to pursue eminent careers and the Scott brothers, whose father was a coal fitter, typified the rise to prominence from humble beginnings. William, the eldest brother, studied diligently and became an authority on maritime law. For his efforts he was elevated to the status of Lord Stowell and his name was given to the street which is now in the Chinese quarter of modern Newcastle. However, it was his younger brother who made the bigger impact, and the city's magnificent Eldon Square [now a shopping mall] would commemorate his name. John Scott rose to the rank of Lord Chancellor of England, head of the judiciary and Leader of the House of Lords.

Scott, who accepted the title of Lord Eldon, did not have a promising start to his career. In his youth he eloped with the daughter of a Newcastle merchant who was adamant that no son of a coal fitter would enter into his family. Scott's future wife was Bessie Surtees, and her house, one of the oldest on the quayside, displays a plaque by an upstairs window to commemorate her escape. John Scott was a contemporary of Cuthbert Collingwood and he wrote:

'Collingwood and I were class fellows at Newcastle. We were placed at the school because neither his father nor mine could afford to place us elsewhere.'

Lord Eldon was with George III when the king received Collingwood's famous dispatch after

Bessie Surtees House

Trafalgar which reported victory and the death of Nelson. The monarch remarked on the grace and style of the letter and his Chancellor said that the Vice-Admiral and himself had sat together with the Rev Moises and that it was he, their teacher, who was the influence for the elegant, expressive writing. Collingwood would have agreed with his classmate's assessment and acknowledged his headmaster's influence. He retained his life-long love of literature and poetry, and as his naval correspondence and personal letters demonstrate, Collingwood had a masterful grasp of the English language.

It is interesting to reflect on the teaching approach young Collingwood received during the Moises' regime which ran from 1748 to 1787. On the school site, the old hospital chapel was the 'classroom' with the headmaster and senior scholars occupying the chancel. An usher, on a raised platform at the east end of the nave, could survey the entire school population which numbered about thirty boys. An ex-scholar, Benjamin Green, later one of the city's finest architects, described how the masters would arrive in full academic dress:

> 'Their appearance offered a dignity and decorum that was not lost on the pupils. Prayers were delivered by the masters. A chapter from the New Testament was read by one of the senior boys. Pupils were arranged in classes according to age, there were no separate rooms; we were all in the chapel together. We would go in groups to the master's desk for instruction.'

Rev Moises kept a close check on the progress of his pupils (and masters) and each Thursday he 'heard' the lower classes. He worked hard during the six-day week and he expected the same commitment of his staff and pupils during the daily nine hours of teaching. Even after school hours the work was not over, for their headmaster introduced innovative exercises for the children to complete in their own time - homework! Latin and the Classics were the mainstay of the school timetable but unusually in 1760, Moises insisted that 'English prose composition' be taught and it would seem that young Collingwood had a flair for this subject.

The educational climate at the time was influenced by the writings of the philosopher, John Locke, who proposed that parents be more gentle and sensitive to the needs of their children. Dickens would publish Nicholas Nickleby [1835] in which he exposed the scandalous maltreatment of school children under the master Wackford Squeers at Dotheboys Hall and that was a fair reflection of educational practices in the late 18th Century. Locke suggested more tolerance and 'liberty of thought' and Hugh Moises attracted pupils to the school because he seemed to embrace these humane principles. John Scott recalled that their headmaster 'always tempered necessary severity with affability and kindness'. Nevertheless he was a strict disciplinarian and the future Lord Chancellor confessed that there was an occasion when he was beaten for 'misdemeanours' and on that one particular day he was 'the seventeenth boy that Moises had flogged.'

The Reverend Moises' educational influence would reach beyond the walls of the grammar school and into the town of Newcastle. In February 1793, the headmaster was invited to chair the meeting that led to the formation of the prestigious Literary and Philosophical Society, and as a prominent member he helped to enlarge the library.

In 1761, when Cuthbert was in his twelfth year, he joined the Navy. It was the end of his formal schooling and the beginning of a nautical education that would be a baptism of fire. He sailed out of the River Tyne and into the open sea on board the *Shannon*. Collingwood was fortunate enough to have 'connections', for his mother's sister was married to Captain Braithwaite, the ship's commander, and the young recruit would recall at a later date:

> 'I was under the protection and care of a kind friend and relation, the late Admiral Braithwaite, whose regard for me, and the interest he took in whatever related to my improvement in nautical knowledge, I owe great obligations.'

The ship he joined was a 'ship-of-the-line' frigate with broadside guns that had been developed over three centuries into an economical fighting machine of wood, iron, hemp and canvas and powered by the muscles of the crew and the vagaries of the wind. He learnt elementary seamanship, such as the use of a compass, and he discovered how the ship was navigated. In spite of his age he was thrown, by necessity, into the practical workings of the ship. The twelve year old began high up in the rigging and was taught how to handle the ship's boats, then he would go below and memorise the detailed anatomy of his ship.

To serve as a midshipman on a frigate was every young boy's dream. The seafaring life promised adventure and excitement and even the struggles as outlined in the popular Daniel Defoe novel *Robinson Crusoe* only made the hard naval life seem more appealing. He arrived in the service soon after the 'Year of Victories' (1759) with the memories of the exploits of Edward Hawke in destroying the French fleet in Quiberon Bay. This heralded the end

Learning the ropes

of the Seven Years' War and the British Empire was at its height on land and sea. The navy had attractions for a growing lad, but whilst he literally learnt the ropes, the life afloat in peacetime was often dull and humdrum. His uncle's role was to patrol the oceans protecting ships with British interest but since the Georgian navy had seen off the opposition there was little opportunity to seek the promised fame and fortune.

For a boy to go to sea at such a young age was not considered a hardship, in fact early entry was sought by men of influence for their sons. In the Royal

Hands in the rigging

Navy it was considered a positive advantage, for the sooner a boy could get a placement the better his chances of becoming promoted to the officer ranks; a foothold onto the rising ladder was paramount. Having relations in the service certainly helped and there was an expectation that uncles, nephews and cousins would use their influence to get a boy a post. Young Collingwood did have his moments of homesickness and in later life he recalled how a senior First Lieutenant had taken pity on him and helped dry away his tears. The officer had shown sympathy and the youngster gave him a large piece of plum cake that his mother had packed for him. Collingwood never forgot this small act of kindness and he always showed concern for the boys in his care when he would finally achieve a position of authority.

In 1766, after six years service, Cuthbert had experienced the climatic extremes of the Atlantic, Baltic, Mediterranean and home waters. By now he was considered sufficiently competent and was promoted to midshipman. As a 'middy' he had his own living space, as the name suggests, amidships, on the lower deck, with a bag for his possessions and a hammock on a pair of hooks. 'Living space' was something of a misnomer for the official allowance was the length of the seaman and a width of fourteen inches [36 centimetres] although since half the seamen worked whilst the others slept, their space was usually a more generous twenty-eight inches! As a midshipman, he was recognised as a trainee officer and although Collingwood was barely eighteen, he now had authority over able seamen and old campaigners three times his age. He had the power to order the flogging of men below decks but he never resorted to this dubious privilege.

A year later as a Braithwaite 'follower' he accompanied his captain to his new vessel the *Gibraltar*. This meant he was hand-picked and groomed by his uncle who could select from the crew of his previous ship. He would now spend more time in the Mediterranean before his ship was sent to the Port of Mahon (Minorca) in the Spanish Balearic Isles to

Horatio Nelson's birthplace, a contrast to Cuthbert's quayside origins

Collingwood's hand-drawn cover of the Portland log book

survey the waters and chart the depths. This may not have seemed very exciting work but this was the period when Captain James Cook and the great explorers were creating accurate maps; discovering unheard of horizons; collecting exotic plants and telling of strange creatures in the New World. At this time a contemporary of Collingwood, fellow-Northumbrian, Thomas Bewick, was coming to the end of his apprenticeship as an engraver, and it would be his prints of animals, birds and rural life that would open the eyes of a nation to the beauty and variety of the natural world. His Newcastle workshop would be a hundred metres from Cuthbert's family home.

By 1772, Collingwood had experienced over a decade at sea with his uncle when it was decided that the very experienced midshipman should be seconded to the *Lennox* under Captain Roddam. Roddam was described as 'a fine old Northumbrian tar and one of the most seasoned mariners of his day.' The young man regarded the captain as a friend and although he did not know it at the time, he would marry Roddam's young relative Sarah, but that was almost twenty years into the future. After an uneventful year patrolling the home waters around Portsmouth, Collingwood was sent across the Atlantic to Jamaica in the *Portland* and it was at this time that he met a precocious young midshipman by the name of Horace Nelson. The fifteen year old from Norfolk, (who would re-name himself Horatio) formed an immediate friendship with his fellow seaman from Newcastle in spite of the ten years that separated their ages. Nelson at the time was a junior officer in a merchant vessel trading in the West Indies because his influential Uncle, Captain Maurice Suckling, felt the time at sea would turn him into a real sailor. Life on the merchant craft was different from the Royal Navy regime as there were no punishments and the gap between officers and men was not so wide. The merchantmen could earn good money without the risk of fighting for their lives but ashore they had to be wary. As skilful seaman they were much sought after by the 'press gangs' who roamed the ports and had the authority to capture crew members for the King's Navy. The ruthless gangs might get a sailor drunk, or beat him unconscious, and the victim could wake to find himself on board a ship that might be at sea for two years. Family and friends would be left wondering as to the whereabouts of their loved ones.

Collingwood knew that the merchant fleets despised the Royal Navy but to his credit, when he was in command, he never indulged in the brutal excesses of some of the more infamous officers. He wanted men around him who were willing and able. Collingwood disliked taking on board the reluctant 'impressed' men although he could see the necessity for them when the nation needed sailors to man the fighting ships. At Trafalgar, one third of Nelson's crew on the *Victory* had been press-ganged.

In 1774 the twenty-six-year-old joined Vice-Admiral Graves on the 'fourth-rate' two-decker *Preston* for a tour of duty in American waters. Collingwood had been recommended to this fighting ship-of-the-line by Captain (soon to be Admiral) Roddam and although it was not much bigger than a frigate, it would still be included in any major conflict, and there seemed to be one boiling up. A year earlier the colonists had emptied 342 chests of tea into their harbour at Boston because they had refused to pay the British stamp duty tax. This landmark event that become known as the 'Boston Tea Party' had hastened the United States War of Independence and the *Preston*, along with other warships, was sent to put these rebellious upstarts in their place. The British military leaders confidently declared that the war would be over in a few short weeks but it continued for eight weary years. France and Spain actively supported the American effort and this did not help the situation; they seemed to be gaining vicarious revenge for the past beatings they had suffered at the hands of the British.

Collingwood had joined the navy to see action and at last, after fourteen years service, he would soon be in the thick of it. But it was not a sea battle as he had imagined, for the burgeoning new nation had no navy, so his participation was on dry land. In his cursory account of this period Collingwood wrote:

'It was on this voyage that I was given the rank of lieutenant. I was promoted by Admiral Graves in 1775 on the day the battle was fought at Bunker's Hill, where I was with a party of seamen, supplying the army with what was necessary to them.'

The new lieutenant offers only modest information on the Battle of Bunker's Hill because although it is not remembered today, it would certainly have been familiar to his contemporaries. Collingwood does not elaborate on the conflict, but it was a major battle between the settlers and the British troops. The military were occupying the colonist's port and controlling all passage in and out. The settlers' reaction to this was to bring in 1500 men to dig a system of trenches and barriers around the port which effectively turned the tables and put the harbour under siege from the mainland. Warships attempted to demolish the defences from the sea but the barrage failed as the Americans were too well entrenched. General William Howe, with distinguished service behind him, decided that 3000 regular troops would sort out the unruly rabble with their 'miscellaneous weapons, doubtful

The Battle of Bunkers Hill 1775

discipline and lack of uniform.' But he was wrong. It needed three separate operations and the first two ended in a bloody repulse. At the third attempt, the soldiers, with marine reinforcements from the fleet, managed to winkle out the settlers. It was a terrible struggle as the soldiers faced the hostility of the defenders who, once their ammunition was spent, retaliated fearlessly with bayonets. Collingwood ensured the soldiers had all the powder and shot they needed. In an understatement he described the action as 'fierce'. The final toll was a costly English victory with a loss of 1000 men including 89 commissioned officers. Today a 220 feet high obelisk marks the spot to commemorate an event that the defenders regarded as a glorious resistance. A year later the British withdrew from Boston.

To receive lieutenant status was an important promotion. The lieutenant would take his place at the 'aft' of ship with the commanding officers and the ordinary seaman would be to the fore. There was a saying that went:

'Aft the most honour, forward the better men.'

The notion being that those who gave the orders were the ones who gained the glory but contributed the least. It is a theme that runs throughout all aspects of military and civilian life. However, Collingwood's elevation to lieutenant was earned by his own actions, as well as passing the compulsory written examination. He was promoted for 'conspicuous personal deeds' and was recommended by serving officers. From now on, promotion and advancement would be achieved by merit - at least that was the theory. A selection board at the Admiralty would make collective decisions that were free of favouritism and patronage. Outstanding actions were rewarded by moving men through the ranks, or conversely, errors of judgement by serving officers could result in the abrupt ending of a promising naval career.

The Northumbrian's promotion was an important step and he had the appointment formally confirmed when he returned home to England on the 74-gun *Somerset*. From the City of London, he wrote to his sister, Elizabeth, or Betsy as he called her, and told her of his new status. After years away from home he had hoped for a two or three month break from duty but he explained:

'I am persuaded that if employment is neglected now, it will be very difficult to attain in six months hence.'

This correspondence, dated 22 March 1776, is significant because it is the first letter from his hand to have survived. Collingwood would have written to his family and friends on previous occasions but now there is a sense of family pride in Cuthbert's new promotion to officer seniority and his letters are retained and valued. They would be circulated, as Collingwood intended, and his

A lieutenant

20

important position at the forefront of national events gave his opinions weight and as a consequence his writings had a better chance of survival. In this particular letter he is still smarting from the Bunker's Hill episode and he lays his political views on the line:

'The Mayor, Aldermen and Common Council, petition the King today to cease hostilities against the Americans, and to adopt some mode of accommodation. I am out of all patience with them, and consider them the supporters of a dangerous rebellion, rather than the asserters of the public Liberty.'

Collingwood was not long in finding a position. His personal appeals (via influential relatives) to Lord Sandwich, Head of the Admiralty, were soon rewarded. The recently appointed lieutenant must have been delighted to learn he had been assigned to the *Hornet,* a new sloop of war that was destined for the West Indies. Any joy he may have felt at the placement would have immediately turned sour when he learnt the name of her commander, Robert Haswell. Collingwood's superior was 'odious and unimaginative' and well known in the service for his embittered outlook. Haswell had spent eighteen years on the lieutenant's list and another fourteen as a commander, and although his crew addressed him as 'captain', he never reached the full post captain's rank. A commander wore a single heavy epaulet on his left shoulder - a captain had a matching pair. To achieve the higher position, an officer had to be in charge of a ship large enough to carry the status of full captain; this was the ambition of every aspiring lieutenant, but Haswell had been conspicuously overlooked and had no prospect of 'taking post'.

A sloop of war

It was an extremely unlucky period for Collingwood, for at this time the colonial wars in America were producing rich pickings for the Royal Navy. It was accepted practice during the Georgian period to confiscate enemy vessels and their cargoes as 'prizes' and then to cash them in at the ports. The enemy did not hand over their property without a fight and the taking of the ships would often follow a very bloody encounter. This legal piracy at a time of war was clearly worth it for the returns were very lucrative. Even for a man of Collingwood's sensibilities, the taking of ships was not considered immoral, it was seen simply as a very profitable commercial venture.

The distribution of the prize money was based on a well-established formula so that the men could calculate what their share would amount to. A typically modest capture might be valued at £2,000 and the total would be divided into eight £250 portions. The captain received three eighths although a third of his cut went immediately to the admiral of the squadron - regardless of his superior's involvement. Next the lieutenants and master would share an eighth, then the surgeon, boson, carpenter, master's mates would share another. The pecking order descended to the young midshipmen, warrant officers and marine sergeant who took their cut and finally the ordinary seaman and marines (around fifty on a sloop) would be left to share out the remaining quarter of the proceeds, which could be around £10 a head. [2005 = £1,000].

It was an extremely frustrating period for Collingwood as he was well aware that his family were financially embarrassed by the recent death of his father. A lieutenant's pay was not enough to support a family who were dependant upon him and he felt the responsibility deeply. Had the *Hornet* confiscated just one of the enemy trading ships, it would have given Collingwood the equivalent of two year's salary at a stroke, enough to keep his family back home in relative comfort. In a letter to his brother John he bemoaned his West Indian predicament and the incompetence and indifference of Captain Haswell:

'When possible prizes were sighted he soon left off the ceremony of even chasing them, and allowed them to pass unmolested sometimes within half a gunshot. This is ⸱ country to make a fortune in; all kinds of people are wallowing in their wealth acquired by prizes and we are such an extraordinary exception, that the *Hornet* has become proverbial for its lack of achievement, even the black girls sing of our poverty in their ludicrous songs.'

Haswell was the problem for he had no 'active spirit'. Collingwood sent this letter via the *Lively*, a ship that was homeward bound and he added:

'There is not a man or officer in the ship that would not consider a removal as a kind of promotion. The fatigue I undergo as lieutenant is inconsiderable compared to what I suffer from the insolent manners of this man's strange compound of extravagant pride, and abject meanness. The *Lively* brings this letter. I would to God the *Lively* could bring me also for I am heartily tired of my situation.'

The *Hornet* was a relatively small sloop at around 150 tons and its length was a mere twenty-four metres. In such a confined space a throwaway remark must have seemed like a public statement. In this claustrophobic atmosphere, surrounded by a crew of around eighty, Cuthbert was obliged to carry out orders and instructions that were against his better judgement. Inevitably a row broke out. When the *Hornet* was in port, a court martial was held for three of the crew who had deserted, and Collingwood, with other witnesses, admitted he had not arrived at the proceedings on time:

'We were later in our attendance than we ought to have been; such things will

Self-portrait 1779

happen in the confusion of careening [to turn a ship on one side for repair]. The president expressed himself displeased and then Haswell added a speech so replete with virulence, rancour and animosity that every hearer stood astonished. Every captain present was unknown to us and I determined that I would make him gainsay all that he had said. We represented to the court that an explanation of such a violent outburst should be given in order that we could vindicate our good name. We maintained that his outpourings were groundless as well as malicious. When Haswell was called to account before the court, the man stood confounded and speechless, and when asked the meaning of his declaration, he with an unparalleled effrontery denied every syllable he had advanced before the same assembly: the creature looked less than a man, he was unworthy even of our resentment. Before these captains he has drawn his own picture and strongly pencilled in its deformities.'

Haswell did not forget this humiliation and soon Collingwood found himself facing a court martial on a charge of 'disobedience and a neglect of orders.' The case came up in early 1777 and Collingwood successfully defended himself against the accusations and was acquitted. In what seems to have been an attempt at retaining Haswell's authority, the Court criticised Collingwood for his apparent 'want of cheerfulness' and they recommended him to 'conduct himself with that alacrity which was essentially necessary to His Majesty's Service.' Collingwood probably had a wry smile over these remarks as the advice to 'lighten up' was given by men who did not have to serve under his captain. It must have been a time of great stress for Cuthbert; he was an ambitious seaman and he would have felt genuine concern for his future. The authorities had the power to move Lieutenant Collingwood but they chose to leave him in the *Hornet* for another miserable year, which the Northumbrian seemed to have accepted with fortitude.

Young Horatio Nelson, post captain

In 1778, Admiral Sir Peter Parker was the Commander-in-Chief in the West Indies and from his base in Jamaica he had been watching the progress of Collingwood. The Admiral had been impressed by his eloquent, spirited defence at his Court Martial and he admired his stoicism under pressure. Parker would be remembered in naval circles as a talent spotter; he had the foresight to take Nelson into his flagship and then make him commander of the brig *Badger*. The following summer of 1779, he appointed Horatio Nelson as Post Captain of the *Hinchinbroke* when he was still three months short of his twenty-first birthday. Collingwood was ten years older than Nelson and he seemed to be shadowing the vicar's son from

Norfolk. The Northumbrian would write in later years:

'Whenever Lord Nelson got a step in rank, I succeeded him. First in the *Lowestoffe*, then in the *Badger*, into which I was made a commander in 1779, and afterwards the *Hitchinbroke*, a 28-gun frigate, which made us both Post Captains.'

A Royal Navy frigate

The pattern was to persist right up to Trafalgar. Fortunately the two men were very close and there was never any trace of jealousy from Collingwood concerning Nelson's meteoric rise. They were also quite different in stature and personality. Nelson's tailored clothes at the Maritime Museum in London suggest his height was five feet five inches, others maintain he was a mere five feet two inches - slightly taller than Napoleon Bonaparte. We do know he had a thin wiry frame but he more than compensated for his size with an expansive outgoing personality, full of confidence and self-assurance. Collingwood was a large, introverted man with broad shoulders and a blunt, often stern demeanour. He was modest of his achievements and perhaps this accounted for his slower rise to prominence as he was not one for self-promotion. The new captains were living proof that opposites attracted and they were always drawn to one another's company and shared the same patriotic aims - protection of the nation by ensuring the total supremacy of the British navy.

At the time of their promotions both Nelson and Collingwood were in the West Indies protecting British interests along the eastern seaboard of Central America. Collingwood's orders were to patrol the Mosquito Shore and the Bay of Honduras and to keep a lookout for the American privateers. This area was strange and wild; it was dense with mangrove swamps, savannah and jungle. The hardwood forests attracted a mixture of freebooting loggers, escaped slaves and Mosquito Indians. The British had settlements and so too did Spain but it was an alien climate for Europeans. Letters home told of fever and sickness amongst their crews - especially officers - so that fatalities on the quarterdecks meant that the men who stayed healthy received steady promotion. When Collingwood was made captain of the *Hinchinbroke*, Nelson was transferred to the *Janus*, but the son of the Norfolk clergyman became very ill with fever and almost died. He was immediately sent home to England to recuperate and Collingwood was sent on an expedition into the Spanish Main, which it was hoped would reach the South Seas. It was an ill-informed plan that could not be achieved and Captain Collingwood admitted:

'The navigational difficulties were not to be surmounted by human skill or perseverance... the climate was deadly; no constitution could resist its effects.'

Collingwood overcame the virulent 'Yellow Jack' but he was very fortunate:

'I survived most of my ship's company, having buried in four months, 180 out of the 200 which composed it. Mine was not a singular case, all the ships that were there as long as I suffered in the same degree: the transport ships were not wanted, for the troops they brought were no more; they had fallen, not by the hand of an enemy but sunk under the contagion of the climate.'

After the appalling misery of the Spanish Main he was put in command of the *Pelican*, a 24-gun frigate, which patrolled the waters around Jamaica. Collingwood was soon making up for the barren financial years under Commander Haswell in the *Hornet* for he very quickly captured a French 16-gun frigate *Le Cert*. The frigate had taken possession of the *Blandford* a richly-laden vessel from Glasgow, so Collingwood not only claimed an enemy prize but he had the satisfaction of releasing a British ship from its captors. This action was well received by the Admiralty who praised the men of the *Pelican* 'under circumstances that reflect the highest credit upon the captain and crew.'

A captain

Collingwood's tour of duty was free of incident during the following nine months until August 1781 when good fortune deserted him. The *Pelican* was coasting off the remote islands of the Morant Keys when a tremendous hurricane blew up through the night. So severe was the storm that over 100 vessels had been driven ashore near Port Royal, Jamaica, and two sturdy men-of-war were entirely de-masted. No ship could have avoided the onslaught and the *Pelican* with Collingwood and his crew was dashed onto the rocks and began breaking up. When daylight came, it was apparent that the commander needed to get his men clear of the wreckage, even though the conditions were still cyclonic. Collingwood described the experience:

'The next day, with great difficulty, the ship's company got on shore by rafts, made of the broken yards, and in those small sandy hills, with little food or water, we remained ten days until a boat went to Jamaica, and the *Diamond* frigate came and took us off.'

The loss of the *Pelican* was a grave disappointment for Collingwood but he was not blamed for the shipwreck, far from it, he was praised for his skill in bringing his crew to safety and keeping them disciplined. He had handled a potential Robinson Crusoe situation extremely well and still had the energy and determination to send a boat to the mainland, some thirty-five miles away, so that his marooned crew could be rescued.

A few months later he was back in England and feeling despondent. After three years of misfortune with Haswell, he had suddenly risen to Post Captain but then his luck had changed once more and he had lost the *Pelican*. Now he was in London, single-mindedly looking for a ship and he refused to be diverted by the city's attractions. He wrote to his brother John about the perils on the street - particularly from the womenfolk:

> 'I begin to think the women are more dangerous to encounter than hurricanes, as they do not give so fair a warning. Would I was aboard again! Better wrecked a thousand times at sea, than once ashore.'

At the age of thirty-five he was not about to be 'wrecked' - he was more concerned with another kind of attachment. Collingwood was not alone in seeking employment; it was a time of relative peace and he was aware that he was competing against experienced officers:

> 'There are at least a hundred captains scrabbling for ships, and I believe I may say all the ships for this season are given away except such as fall vacant by chance.'

There would be no bonuses from the capture of prize ships and during periods of inactivity on shore the officers were retained on half-pay but for ambitious men of rank, that was not enough. The ordinary seaman was paid-off after returning from a voyage, and if they were unlucky (like the men on the wrecked *Pelican*) they received nothing - even after months or years at sea.

The Admiralty waiting room. A cartoonist's view of the unemployed officers

In spite of Collingwood's grumbles he was actually quite fortunate for he found himself appointed to the newly-built frigate *Mediator* and heading for Antigua in July 1783 - back to the West Indies. Cuthbert's satisfaction in his appointment was tempered by the shortage of manpower. The high fatality rate in the West Indies' campaigns had depleted the supply of English mariners. The Admiralty offered press-gang crews but he did not welcome this enforced labour. Collingwood would have preferred Tyneside sailors but the skilful keelmen fraternity that he knew so well from boyhood days had paid a levy of £100 to avoid the impressments. As an admiral, he would have north-eastern seamen under his leadership at Trafalgar, but for now he had to make do with any able-bodied men regardless of nationality. It was customary for captains to take their favoured crew with them when promoted but Collingwood's last ship had been the *Pelican* and the officers and men had long since dispersed after the fateful shipwreck. The *Mediator* was new and did not come with an existing crew so any men that he took on board would have to be trained in the ways of their captain and it would be down to Collingwood to bond the disparate group of strangers into an effective team.

Collingwood was also responsible for loading the ship with supplies. Typically he would need casks of beef, pork and butter along with dried soup and the hard-tack biscuits that were ordered by the ton. The purser, who would oversee the provisions on board, had to be consulted and every item of food had to be numbered and countersigned before being packed tightly into the bowels of the ship. Butts of rum were lowered in alongside the great barrels of fresh water although after three weeks into a voyage the water would turn rancid. Food was essential but so too were the armaments. The gunpowder was packed into the copper-lined storerooms at either end of the ship where it was handled with great care. A candle sealed behind a glass recess would illuminate the room and the copper ensured that there would be no unwelcome sparks. The iron 'shots' would then be distributed on board and as well as the conventional round balls there would be chain, bar, grape and a variety of other deadly projectiles. The cannons needed sponges, pails, matches, wads and priming irons and a reserve supply of replacements. Into the holds would go the ropes, blocks and tackle, sails and timbers - everything that was needed to equip and repair the ship in its line of duty. It was expected that Royal Navy commanders would be frugal in their demands from the Admiralty stores; careful records were kept and any spendthrifts in the fleet would be censured. Collingwood was well known for

making savings and looking after the 'King's stores'. In the heat of battle at Trafalgar, he famously called over Lieutenant Clavell, and together they rescued a sail on the *Royal Sovereign* that had been shot to shreds because Collingwood felt it could be repaired at a later date. It was also true that economical masters had a greater chance of promotion; profligacy did not pay.

Admiralty House c.1790

As he waited for his ship to be loaded up he encountered another problem - toothache. However, Cuthbert was not prepared to allow physical discomfort to hold him back. With typical stoicism he wrote to his sister telling of his remedy for the raging molar:

'The tooth was so painful to me that I just had to have it taken out. On its removal I had the hollow part filled with caddie lead then put it back in again. Tomorrow I hope it will be as good a tooth as any that I have.'

The incident demonstrated Collingwood's resourcefulness and ability to find the right solution to a problem, although it was common practice in the Georgian period for the wealthy to have their dentist/barber pull out a bad tooth and have it replaced in the same spot by a healthy tooth. A rich patient would have a tooth extracted whilst a destitute child lay alongside and the dentist would select a replacement from the youngster's mouth. It was a source of income for the poor but it was grisly employment with short-term prospects.

Collingwood eventually left the English shore anticipating an easy voyage. A peace treaty had been signed with France and Spain; American independence had been formally recognised so there would be no prospect of prize money. However, if Collingwood had been expecting a trouble-free trip, he was very much mistaken. Before the War of Independence the British colonies in the West Indies had happily traded with the people of North America because they were all serving under the King. The war had changed all that, and by declaring itself independent, America had become in effect, a foreign power. Now, according to the strict letter of the long-established Navigation Laws, only British-registered vessels could trade with her colonies. Sir Richard Hughes was the governor of the region and he ignored this century-old directive and 'winked his eye' at the illegal trading. Collingwood was not prepared to allow it and on the afternoon of 15th December 1784 he intercepted an American vessel that was heading for the harbour at Antigua. He asked her business and the captain claimed he needed to enter the port to repair the main mast - a common excuse to gain access and discharge their cargo. Collingwood sent his own carpenter on board to examine the defect and he concluded that the damage was slight and that the repair could be carried out by the *Mediator* in open sea, which it was. The ship never made it into port and this aroused the anger of the captain and the whole of the trading community, not to mention the embarrassed Governor Hughes. He wrote to Collingwood saying:

A ship's carpenter

'You are on no account to hinder, or prevent such foreign ship or vessel from going in [the harbour] or to interfere in her subsequent proceedings.'

Cuthbert had no respect for the governor, who, according to Nelson 'bowed and scraped too much.' Sir Richard Hughes famously wore a piratical patch over his eye but he evidently lost his sight, not in battle, but in the Leeward Islands whilst attempting to kill a cockroach with a table fork. Collingwood wrote that 'the easy temper' of the governor made him a dupe for some artful people:

'The Admiral's compliance suited every prominent planter, merchant and Custom House official on the station, but not the interest of Great Britain.'

Nelson, who had followed Collingwood to Antigua and was the senior officer, backed his friend up to the hilt. He wrote home and informed Lord Sydney, the

Minister responsible for Colonial Affairs, of their actions in blocking the illegal trade. The reply from England firmly supported their naval viewpoint. Nelson and Collingwood were joined by Wilfred, Cuthbert's younger brother, who was captain of the *Rattler*, and the three of them were vigilant in the carrying out of their duty. The traders on both sides were furious as were the old establishment at the interference of these young upstarts. Hughes told Nelson:

'Old gentlemen are not in the habit of taking advice from young gentlemen.'

Nelson replied:

'I have the honour of being as old as the Prime Minister [William Pitt was 27] and I think myself as capable of commanding one of His Majesty's ships as that minister is of governing a state.'

He would later write in a confidential letter:

'The Admiral and all about him are great ninnies; they are a sad set of geese. Had it not been for Collingwood, it would have been the most disagreeable station that ever I saw.'

The hostility and isolation the captains experienced at Antigua would have been intolerable but for John Moutray, the sympathetic Commissioner for the Naval Board, or more accurately, his wife. At this time Cuthbert was thirty-seven and Horatio was a decade younger but both were besotted by the young Mary Moutray. She seemed to bring out the best in Cuthbert; she penetrated his reserved and diffident nature so that his natural wit, charm and originality of thought, began to surface. Mary confided: 'He is a most attractive companion to those who know him well.' Cuthbert was admitted to her boudoir and helped curl her hair and he would stand beside her to turn the sheets of music as she played the piano. He was tall, strong and became, as she put it 'a beloved brother in our house.' Mary was pretty, funny, clever and resolutely faithful to her elderly husband. Collingwood wrote her poems and Nelson composed love letters; she even encouraged the captains to make portraits of each other. The portraits are

Nelson by Collingwood

Collingwood by Nelson

in the Nelson room at the British Maritime Museum at Greenwich and Collingwood is depicted in silhouette with his long hair in a 'queue'; Nelson is framed in profile wearing an ill-fitting wig. He shaved his hair off because his scalp itched unbearably when he was in a malarial sweat, although the ludicrous yellow wig did not help his appearance. The Moutray home was a haven of peace and affection; both men visited as often as they could and it became a meeting place where the two captains bonded their friendship. While they were both in Antigua the 61-year-old Commissioner took ill and Mary had to return to England for the sake of her husband's health. Nelson and Collingwood were bereft. When Mary was leaving she presented Cuthbert with a purse of netting that she had made for him. In response, he wrote her a whimsical poem:

Your net shall be my care, my dear,
For length of time to come,
While I am faint and scorching here,
And you rejoice at home.

To you belongs the wondrous art
To shed around you pleasure;
New worth to best of things impart
And make of trifles, treasure.

In the Georgian period, tales of unrequited love were very fashionable, so the young seamen were not out of step with the times.

Wilfred did not seem to have an outlet for his emotions and he was usually depicted as being very earnest and serious. When he was thirty-four, Cuthbert wrote to his sister saying that 'Wilfred is always called old Collingwood and has been taken for fifty.' He added that:

> 'Influential people have remarked on his diligence, attention and the good order of his ships; his character has been talked about, so it is highly likely that he will make his mark.'

Wilfred did make an impact, and as commander of the sloop *Rattler* did sterling work under Nelson. By late summer 1786 Collingwood had returned home, and it was here that the family received a sad letter from Nelson dated 3rd May 1787, that told of the death of Wilfred, at the age of thirty-seven. The cause of death was not given but it may have been tuberculosis; although others maintain Wilfred had worn himself out with

Wilfred Collingwood: the only known portrait

the responsibility of command. 'He left this life' wrote Nelson 'without a groan or struggle.' Prince William and Nelson had both cried for the loss of a 'faithful servant of the service and most excellent officer.' Soon after, Wilfred Collingwood's effects were delivered by boat up the River Tyne to Newcastle; the shrunken, scanty parcel contained the possessions of a promising young officer of no private means, and a letter of condolence.

By 1786 there seemed to be peace on the other side of the Atlantic and the French were occupied with an internal revolution, the impact of which, would soon spread and dominate their nation for years to come. The British fleet were not required and they were laid up in port although some were used to transport convicts to Australia. Others were simply used as prison ships to contain the criminal elements that seemed to be infected by the lawless activities of their Gallic neighbours. For the time being the British Isles were free of enemy threat and Cuthbert Collingwood could come home from his overseas posting. Throughout his fifty years at sea he would know only three prolonged periods ashore and this was one of them. From 1786 to 1790 he found himself on dry land, away from his seafaring companions, and having to adjust to unaccustomed surroundings after 26 years of almost continuous service. He would write of this time:

> 'I was in Northumberland, making my acquaintance with my own family, to whom I had hitherto been, as it were, a stranger.'

He used his vacation years productively for he met Sarah, of Charlotte Square, Newcastle, the daughter of John Erasmus Blackett, the city's Mayor and a friendship developed. Cuthbert Collingwood was thirty-eight years of age when he went into temporary retirement and it would be almost five years before his services were called upon once more.

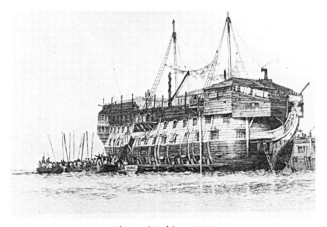

A convict ship c.1788

CAPTAIN COLLINGWOOD
The Heat of the Battle

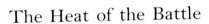
To honour we call you, not press you like slaves.

If there was peace on the home front, the turbulence was building in mainland Europe. In 1789 there was the 'Storming of the Bastille' and this gesture of breaking into the Paris gaol and releasing a handful of inmates was seen as a symbol of freeing the people from oppression. The succeeding monarchs and their leaders had not served their subjects well and the palace at Versailles was regarded as the supreme indulgence when there was poverty in the cities and famine in the country.

It was an Englishman, Tom Paine, who contributed to the unrest with his *The Rights of Man* publication although the British establishment did not share his opinions. Whilst they were happy to see France preoccupied with internal disputes, the monarchy had no desire to see the revolutionary fervour spread to this island. Paine believed that Parliament should be a genuine representation of the people and not just for those who could afford to buy themselves a comfortable niche in the seat of power. At the height of the French Revolution, Paine publicly declared that we should ally ourselves to the old enemy France and thereby do away with the need for an expensive naval fleet. He maintained that there would be enormous savings that would reduce personal taxes. What would Captain Collingwood have made of that declaration? It was a popular argument with the reformers but the young Prime Minister, William Pitt, and his government, were alarmed at such a proposal. The 200,000 copies that were sold of *The Rights of Man* made Paine a wealthy man but it also implied that he had popular support for his views. He would eventually become a respected member of the French Assembly (the people's parliament) but his enthusiasm for the cause diminished during the bloody 'Reign of Terror' when he was lucky to escape the guillotine's cutting edge.

Meanwhile Collingwood's reputation as a respected captain was not forgotten. In

Thomas Paine

1790 he was given the command of the *Mermaid* and he returned to the West Indies to cruise around on a peaceful tour of duty. Nelson was not so lucky, he would have to wait another two years for a ship. He had married Fanny Nisbet in 1787, an English widow with a young son, whom he had met during his American posting. Fanny had been staying with her rich uncle, John Herbert, in a beautiful Caribbean mansion where she managed the house and looked after his guests. Nelson brought her back to England but in his unemployed situation he was reduced to living in rented rooms in London. Her future financial prospects would be secure but three years after their marriage, Nelson was struggling to support her. He wrote to his friend: 'Dear Coll, What have I done to be overlooked?' In some quarters of the Admiralty there was a feeling that Nelson was something of a troublemaker and his intransigence at Antigua seemed to confirm this.

Collingwood did not return to the British shores until April 1791 but within two months of stepping onto the mainland he married Sarah Blackett and they set up home in the county town of Morpeth, fifteen miles from his Newcastle birthplace. In spite of his time away from England, he was very fond of rural Northumberland and he planted acorns at every opportunity. A love of his country and commitment to the nation's naval superiority became something of a personal crusade. Collingwood was aware that the Royal Navy 'heart of oak' ships needed the necessary timber to replenish their ageing fleet and he contributed to this cause by his acorn-planting campaign. During the Georgian period, when it took two thousand oak trees to create a single warship, there was always a shortage of

Lady Sarah Collingwood, Cuthbert's wife

timber in the British Isles. Cuthbert practiced what he preached and acquired land in the Cheviot foothills at College Valley in Northumberland and created plantations there but the soil and weather produced a slow-growing, unproductive crop. His personal fertility was more successful and in time Sarah would gave birth to two girls, Sarah junior and Mary Patience. Cuthbert would be a concerned and considerate parent, although mostly by letter from distant horizons.

By 1793, the French were becoming troublesome and war was declared on Britain yet again. Collingwood was required once more and he left Morpeth to join up with an old friend, Rear Admiral George Bowyer. He was immediately given the command of the *Prince*, a huge vessel with three decks and ninety-eight guns. This was a bright new addition to the British naval forces but to Collingwood's dismay it was 'the most miserable sailer in the fleet, for ever in the rear.' The sheer size of the *Prince* made her cumbersome and unwieldy in the ocean. The *Prince* would eventually become the first man-of-war ship to be cut in half and made longer but in spite of her improvements she was as ponderous as ever. Collingwood, as Flag Captain to the Admiral, was happy to transfer to the *Barfleur*, which was an older ship, but it 'handled well'.

At home there was a growing uncertainty about the threat from across the Channel, or German Ocean as the maps would describe it. There was genuine anxiety that the French would overrun the British Isles. The stories of the bloody revolution made chilling reading and the population along the south-east coast lived in fear and trepidation. At first there was sympathy for the downtrodden French population that had risen up against a corrupt and unfeeling monarch. There was a hearty welcome from democratic reformers on this side of the water for the downfall of a system that was cruel and unjust. However, opinion changed when the revolution imprisoned King Louis XVI, and his wife, Marie Antoinette, and threatened them with execution. They would

soon face the guillotine but before that the rapacious revolutionaries hunted down and murdered two thousand opponents of the new republic in a single month in September 1792. It has been said that many of the victims were officers from the French Navy who were seen as upholding and representing the King's authority. At a stroke, the rebels wiped out the cream of their naval power and fatally weakened their maritime strength.

'Madame Guillotine' in the Reign of Terror

Collingwood's response to the activities across the channel was predictable. He was a conservative at heart and deplored the revolution:

> 'If the French people are not all mad, I pity most sincerely those who have yet retained their senses. I hope the miseries of France will be such a lesson to the patriots of this country so as to teach them the true value of our form of government, which offers the means of happiness to all who have the nature and disposition to enjoy it.'

Cuthbert illustrated his opinions in a letter to Nelson:

> 'There are great commotions in our neighbourhood at present. The seamen at Shields have embarked themselves, to the number of 1,200 or 1,400, with a view to compel the owners of the coal-ships to advance their wages; and, as is generally the case when they consider themselves the strongest party, their demand has been exorbitant. Application was made to the Government

for such assistance as the remedy of this evil might require. They have sent the *Drake* and *Martin* sloops to join the *Racehorse*, which was here before, and some troops of dragoons, whose presence I hope, will dispose the Johnnies to peace without having occasion to act. But the times are turbulent; and the enthusiasm for liberty is raging even to madness. The success of the French people will lead to misery here and the undoubted consequence of any commotion will disturb our present most excellent Constitution.'

The revolution fervour spread to the French borders and the zeal and numbers of the armed working classes overwhelmed their neighbours. Holland, Prussia, Austria and Spain were compelled to sign peace treaties and unite with the French leadership so that Great Britain found itself increasingly isolated. The only access to Britain was by sea and the nation pinned its hopes on the Royal Navy fleet and their commanders. A head to head battle with the Europeans was imminent.

When the confrontation eventually took place in 1793, Flag Captain Collingwood in the *Barfleur* was very influential in the battle that King George III would officially declare as the 'Glorious First of June'. The contents of a letter, dated 5th June, to his father-in-law Mr Blackett, described how the British had triumphed against their old adversary. Collingwood was fully aware, that by having the Mayor of Newcastle as his correspondent, his words would be widely circulated. His detailed account was written in the aftermath of the conflict when the guns had ceased firing and the victory could be considered with informed reflection. It is still difficult to read Collingwood's powerful first-hand account without feeling the immediacy of the excitement and horror that was still fresh in his mind:

'I feel myself very unequal to describe a battle, unlike anything that perhaps ever happened before, for we had three days of fighting before we were crowned with the victory. It was defeat for the enemy and we put to flight a fleet superior to our own in numbers, and sent out for the express purpose of destroying us. It was on the 29th May, little Sarah's birthday, that the full French fleet were sighted and minor skirmishes began.'

Fog then descended and the full battle took place 48 hours later on June 1st. The fear and foreboding that affected every man on both sides must have been palpable as Collingwood graphically wrote:

'At dawn, we made our approach on the enemy, then drew up, dressed our ranks, and it was about eight when the Admiral

The 'Glorious First of June'

made the signal for each ship to engage her opponent, and bring her close to action, and then down we went under a crowd of sail, and in a manner that would have animated the coldest heart in the most intrepid enemy. Our orders told us which ship to engage and we had to go through the fire of the French Admiral's ship and two others. We received their broadsides and the full discharge of their guns two or three times before we fired a shot.'

It was ten o'clock in the morning and it says much for Collingwood's character that he could reflect on their predicament with humour and determination. He observed to his admiral that:

'Back in England our wives were going to church, but I thought the peal we should ring about the Frenchmen's ears would outdo their bells.'

It took a great deal of courage to hold back from the barrage that was assailing them but they were determined to wait until they were close enough to have the maximum impact. It is not difficult to visualise the terrified crew with the gunners lying low, on standby, waiting for the order to 'Fire!' They must have wondered as they were under attack whether they would still be alive to retaliate – such was the battering that the *Barfleur* was receiving. Collingwood observed:

'Lord Howe began his fire some time before we did; and he is not in the habit of firing soon.'

Then the moment came.

'We got very near indeed and began such a fire as would have done you good to have heard. During the whole action the most exact order was preserved.'

The crew had kept to their posts and released broadside after broadside in rapid succession. The commanders were aft on the bridge and were exposed to fire from the French military marksmen that were sniping down at them from the enemy rigging. After ten minutes Admiral Bowyer was wounded and Captain Collingwood caught him in his arms before he fell:

'The first lieutenant was slightly wounded by the same shot and I thought that I was in a fair way of being left on the deck by myself.'

Collingwood was relieved to see the lieutenant emerge from below with his head wound dressed. He continued his description:

'A call came from the forecastle to say that the enemy ship was sinking and three cheers broke out. The French vessels in our vicinity were taken, apart from the French Admiral who was driven out of the line and fled with the battered remains of his fleet leaving behind seven of their fine ships as a prize for the victors.'

The *Barfleur* did her duty splendidly, by breaking through the enemy line and being involved in the

Lord Howe

thick of the fighting. Collingwood had the additional burden of losing Admiral Bowyer (whose leg was later amputated) and he, as flag captain took over the direction of the ship.

The conflict led to the death and severe injuries of many of the fleet leaders, and whilst it ended the careers of men in authority, it did mean that Collingwood and his peers would move up the ranks to replace them. Promotion was via the crude 'dead man's shoes' elevation through the system. However, Collingwood's compassion was genuine as he reported that 'We had nine men killed on our ship and twenty-two with severe wounds.' But a naval man to the last he added:

'Yet our masts etc are all in their places although they are much damaged. This has been the severest action that has ever been fought in our time, perhaps ever. It did not last much more than two hours when ten of the enemy ships were de-masted and only two of ours. We understand their orders were to give no quarter; and indeed they fought as if they expected none.'

Collingwood had spent many hours training his men in gunnery practice and during the battle this had paid dividends - literally. The prize ships gave the men a handsome return for their efforts. The seamen had been grimly fighting for their lives but the prospect of a pot of money at the end of it was also a powerful motivation; the Navy was aware that this subtle form of bribery would make the men ferocious opponents.

It had been a decisive victory in which Collingwood had played a significant role and he was well satisfied with his day's work. He could not have given more in the battle so it came as a great disappointment to discover that he had not been mentioned in the Commander-in-Chief, Lord Howe's dispatch. His own Admiral Bowyer was said to have 'fought with distinction' and a number of other captains were held up for 'special notice' but not Collingwood. Howe went on to say:

'These selections should not be construed to the disadvantage of other commanders who may have been equally deserving, although I am not able to make a statement of their merits'

That made matters worse. Collingwood wrote: 'The appearance of that letter nearly broke my heart.' The Northumbrian was not a vain man but he did have a strong sense of justice and he believed that he had been unfairly overlooked. For not receiving the public praise he felt he deserved, Collingwood interpreted Howe's neglect as an official slight and was bitterly disappointed. Peerages and knighthoods were distributed amongst senior officers and junior admirals were created baronets; almost all the captains received the cherished gold medals that were especially struck to mark the victory. Cuthbert Collingwood received nothing.

Flag Captain Collingwood approached Sir Roger Curtis, whom it was believed was responsible for 'naming the conspicuous actions' of the leaders of the fleet, on behalf of Admiral Howe. Curtis, who was not a popular man, told Collingwood that he 'made the selection the Admiral was pleased to make' and that he must stop somewhere. Captain Packenham, one of those mentioned in despatches for recognition, was outspoken in his defence of his fellow seaman:

'If Collingwood hasn't deserved a medal, then neither have I; for we were together the whole day.'

Admiral Bowyer was in no doubt as to the merit of his captain as he wrote to Admiral Roddam six months after the 'Glorious First of June':

'I do not know a more brave, capable, or a better officer, in all respects, than Captain Collingwood. I think him a very fine character; and I told Lord Chatham when he was in Portsmouth, that if ever he had to look for a First Captain or a Commander-in-Chief, I hoped he would remember that I pledged myself that he would not find a better man than our friend Collingwood.'

In July, Collingwood made the long trip home to Morpeth, 'just to catch a glimpse of my darlings.' He was met by his wife Sarah on the road and for forty-eight hours he put aside (for the time being) his simmering disappointment. Cuthbert had hoped for a longer stay but a message from the Admiralty recalled him, and the man of duty, immediately set off on the 320-mile journey to London. The trip to the north had been worth it as his letter to his close friend Dr Carlyle verifies:

A Collingwood miniature portrait

'I am delighted with my little daughters, who quite met my expectations. Sarah seems to possess all the sweet gentleness of her mother; mildness and sensibility are marked in all her childish actions. That child will be a comfort if we live old. Mary Patience, however, possesses more fire, a quicker temper; she will be a spirited dame, but with proper training and the example she will have ever before her, I doubt not we shall have an inexhaustible source of joy. How thankful I am for such blessings.'

On arrival at the capital he wrote to Sarah's uncle, Sir Edward Blackett, and his tone was quite a contrast to the family letter. It still rankled with Collingwood that he had been overlooked and true to his forthright Northumbrian code he sought out his Commander-in-Chief:

'I went yesterday to visit Lord Howe and he received me very graciously and hoped my ship would soon be in a condition to join his fleet. As soon as the polite niceties were out of the way, I told him how much I had been disappointed and hurt, after giving all the exertion I was capable of, yet not having obtained that testimony of his approbation which he had given to others, and which I hoped for.'

It seemed that Lord Howe was anxious to change the subject and he attempted to alter the course of their conversation. Collingwood's brave, outspokenness had left Lord Howe very uncomfortable for he added:

'I believe his Lordship heartily wishes his letter had never been wrote.'

In spite of the apparent snub, Collingwood continued to serve his country and it must have been a relief to be spared a Caribbean trip in favour of cruising the Mediterranean, where he remained in command of the *Excellent* for eighteen months. Both Collingwood and his men remained healthy and fit. His exercises and gun drill were practised repeatedly even though it seemed unnecessary when they were unlikely to face their foe at sea. Collingwood was a disciplinarian and a stickler for regimentation - a source of admiration by many but an irritation by others who grew tired of his working schedules.

The 'Glorious First of June' had left the enemies in no doubt that Britannia, for the time being, held the upper hand although the Royal Navy did not have control of the Mediterranean ports.

Horatio Nelson, to his great disappointment, had missed out on the June victory but his posting to Naples the previous year had not been uneventful. It was here that he met the British ambassador Sir William Hamilton and his attractive young wife, Emma. The Hamilton's were also friends of King Ferdinand and Queen Maria Carolina who was the sister of Marie Antoinette. Horatio was made most welcome and he even persuaded the king to supply 2,000 Sicilian soldiers to help the British in their defence of the naval station at Toulon. The additional reinforcements, however, were inadequate; the relentless French revolutionary army pushed into the port from the mainland and overwhelmed the occupying force. The British were driven out and they left the local

Nelson's favourite portrait of Emma

population to the mercy of the marauding army. One of the artillery lieutenants was a young Napoleon Bonaparte and he was instrumental in seeing off the Royal Navy.

Defeated, the fleet had to look elsewhere for a naval base. Nelson sailed south-east to the island of Corsica (Napoleon's birthplace) and attempted to remove the French who were holding out at a fort in Calvi. He landed his marines and as he looked towards the battlements, an enemy shell exploded amongst the defensive sandbags nearby. Horatio was not badly wounded but the scattering dirt and stones blinded him in his right eye. He did not lose his eye but from that moment he maintained he could only 'distinguish light from darkness, and as to all purpose of use, the eye is gone.' He added:

'It confined me for one day, when, thank God, I was enabled to attend to my duty. I feel the want of it; but such is the chance of war, it was within a hair's breadth of taking off my head.'

Later, when Nelson continued to serve in the Mediterranean, he had a green shade made for his good *left* eye to protect it from the sun's glare and this led to confusion amongst the portrait artists of the day as to which eye was the blind one.

Nelson had lost half of his sight a month after the 'Glorious First' but by the time Cuthbert arrived in the peaceful Tuscan waters in August he had learned to live with the discomfort. He made contact with the *Excellent's* captain and expressed his delight to be united with his old friend. Nelson wrote to 'Dear Coll' and told him that his command in the Mediterranean was pleasant but that the current political climate had left his fleet inactive. Nelson was a man of action and he knew Collingwood was a like-minded captain. Horatio expected Britain to make peace with Spain but he did not trust the Dons and he was inclined to give them a 'drubbing'. He and Collingwood would have happily sailed into the Spanish ports and destroyed their fleet because they both believed that the Spaniards would rise again, and Britain's naval supremacy, gained after the 'Glorious First', would be lost. They were right to distrust Spain but the politicians were unwilling to attack a nation that appeared to be friendly.

In mainland Europe, the French army went from strength to strength and their strong-arm tactics persuaded Spain to join their invasion force, as Collingwood and Nelson had predicted. Spain were master shipbuilders and they had amassed a colossal fleet of 28 ship-of-the-line, including the four-decker *Santissima Trinadada* with its132 guns - the largest ship afloat. They also weighed in with 6 three-deckers, two ships of 84 guns and eighteen of 74 guns. Their admiral, Juan de Cordova, intended to team up with the 30 ship-of-the-line French fleet which were concentrated at Brest to create a force of almost sixty deadly warships. Their united firepower would have been irresistible. Perhaps the Spanish commander recalled the Armadas that came to Elizabethan England exactly two centuries earlier. Certainly, the ultimate plan was to wipe out the weaker (in numbers) British fleet and open up the island nation to an unimpeded invasion. The invincible French soldiers were told they would soon be landing in Britain and would conquer the island as they had in 1066. The Royal Navy had other ideas. Collingwood was in command of the *Excellent* when he wrote a letter to his wife dated 17th February 1797:

'My dearest Sarah

I am sure you will be glad to hear from me after such a day as we had on the 14th (Valentine's Day). It was indeed a glorious one, and it seldom falls to the lot of any man to share in such a triumph. First, my love, I am as well as I ever was in my life, and have pretty well got the better of my fatigue. Now for history.'

Collingwood described how the fleet, with 15 ship-of-the-line, were cruising off Cape St Vincent when they received news that the Spanish fleet of 27 warships and 12 frigates, were in the neighbourhood. The British were outnumbered by over two-to-one but the Commander-in-Chief, Admiral Sir John Jervis signalled to his fleet that he 'determined to attack them' and told his men 'a victory is necessary for the welfare of our country.' It was an unequal contest. The odds were heavily stacked against the commander but as Collingwood put it:

'Should we not be grateful to him, who had such confidence in his fleet, that he thought no force too great for them.'

Jervis was a very flexible commander and was not in favour of the rigid tradition of facing the foe rather like duellists. To exchange gunfire with the enemy was not to the advantage of the British navy. Rather than an ordered battle Jervis preferred a melee which exactly suited the manoeuvrability of the British ships and the close rapid skills of the gunners. Collingwood, the master gunner, was delighted with this tactic:

'Soon after daylight we saw them very much scattered, while we were a compact little body. We flew to them as a hawk to his prey, passed through them in their disordered state and separated them into two distinct parts then tacked [turned] upon their largest division.'

The British Commander-in-Chief positioned himself to square up to the front of the enemy line but unfortunately for Jervis his own ships had not yet put themselves into the gap between the enemy fleet. The planned manoeuvre was incomplete and the Spanish second division were bearing down on him to support their leaders. The crucial gap had not been closed and it looked as though Jervis in *Victory* would be overwhelmed by the enemy. The British ships could see the danger but they were powerless to help as they had received the strict 'order of battle' instructions from their commander. In the late 18th century, orders from above were sacrosanct; no subordinate officer would dare to act on their own initiative. The consequences of disobeying a superior would unquestionably end up with a court-martial and probable disgrace - or worse. Commodore Horatio Nelson, in his ship the *Captain*, saw the danger and without hesitation, made a decision. He refused to allow the perilous situation to develop; he did the unthinkable. His ship was the last but two in the line, but Nelson broke out, overtaking his fleet and single-handedly drove his quicker vessel directly at the enemy. Leaving the line was usually seen as an act of cowardice but in this case Nelson's action was extremely brave. His unique tactic blocked the enemy pathway and completely disrupted their movements. It took tremendous courage for Nelson to defy Admiral Jervis, a man who was renowned as an extreme disciplinarian. The near-suicidal mission led to the *Captain's* sails and rigging being shot through and her steering wheel was smashed, which was not surprising as seven ships began firing at Nelson,

The Battle of St Vincent

including three with over 100 guns and the 132 awesome cannons of the *Santissima Trinidada*. The numbers involved in attempting to eradicate the *Captain* actually proved to be a blessing, for after facing the first broadside, the British vessel was obscured by smoke and the massed enemy ships fired into each other in the confusion.

Admiral Jervis watched from afar in disbelief as he observed the *Captain* disappear in billows of gun-smoke as she engaged the Spanish ships. To the commander's credit, he immediately understood Nelson's actions and he ordered Cuthbert Collingwood in *Excellent* and Tom Troubridge in *Culloden* to go to Nelson's assistance. Both men were close friends of Horatio and they were delighted to join the fray. Collingwood made straight for the *Santissima Trinadada* for he had seen with that quick eye which made him a genius of naval warfare, that if the Spanish van - and the largest ship in the world - could be held in check, it would give the rest of the British sail-of-the-line time to execute their turn and face up to the enemy. The *Excellent* was soon up with Nelson and her crew now proved themselves in close action. For Collingwood, all those hours of gun drill were put into practice. It was generally accepted that the Newcastle-born seaman had brought the art of gun warfare to the highest peak of efficiency and his warship poured broadside after broadside into the enemy. The support for *Captain* was invaluable and the enemy were forced to transfer their attention to the barrage of shots from *Excellent.*

The *Excellent* had 74 guns but one broadside only used half her capacity of 37. All the canons could not be fired together as this would create a mighty kickback effect for the whole ship, so it had to be a rapid continuous fire of one gun after another in very quick succession. Once fired, the gun's recoil would be contained by breeching ropes and the team of at least six men would stand well clear. The gun was essentially an iron tube sealed at one end and into the muzzle a wet sponge, attached to a rammer, was plunged in and turned three times to douse any sparks and to cool down the barrel. A packed gunpowder charge was rammed home and young boys known as 'powder monkeys' delivered this to the gun at each firing. It was their job to run back and forth from their post to the copper-lined powder stores at either end of the ship. After the powder came the cannonball or chosen shot, then a wad of rags were packed into place for maximum velocity. The gun was 'run out' through the ship's ports, and at the breach, or firing end, a spike was pushed into a touchhole vent that passed through the muzzle to penetrate the pack of gunpowder. More gunpowder was sprinkled into the cavity and this was ignited by a flintlock that sent showers of sparks onto the powder - this created the explosion that sent the projectile towards its deadly destination. The flintlock was operated by the chief gunner, using a lanyard or short line, and it was he who sighted the cannon along its length and shouted instructions to seaman on either side of the barrel who levered the heavy mass of iron into the correct firing alignment. On 'Fire!' he would pull the string, or light the powder with a taper, and with a roar and cloud of smoke, the shot left the barrel. The explosion was deafening; like a great hammer hitting a stone at half-second intervals. At the same moment, the gun and carriage leapt violently back on its iron wheels to be restrained by the ropes and before it settled, the wet sponge rammer was once again plunged into the muzzle. As battle raged, the guns became so hot they could scarcely be touched. It was a highly dangerous occupation, for the crews and for the enemy but Collingwood's men had perfected the art, and science, so that they were able to fire a round repeatedly in less than a minute. Spanish gun drill was slow and it was said that Collingwood's gunners could fire off five rounds in the time it took for her opponents to release one round which seems an exaggeration, but for the enemy, five minutes for a single broadside was considered the acceptable norm.

In the heat of the battle, Nelson, in spite of commanding a ship that had lost it's steering, fortuitously drifted into close contact with the Spanish *San Josef*. He ordered his men to fasten onto her and called for 'Boarders!' As a commodore of high rank, Nelson was a valuable asset to the Royal Navy and he would not have been expected to take part in the hand-to-hand fighting. The loss of sight to his right eye should have made him cautious but it seems nothing was going to stop him from leading the charge against the *San Josef*. A detachment of marines climbed on board, and the depleted enemy crew could not prevent the onslaught. The Spanish brigadier fell during the brief exchanges of gunfire and 'within a few moments' the *San Josef* surrendered and was in British hands. Nelson captured this 'prize' in his own ship that the enemy had practically destroyed. He later explained:

> 'At this time the *Captain* had lost her fore topmast and not a sail, shroud or rope was left; her wheel was shot away and the vessel was incapable of further service in line or in the chase.'

But still his work was not finished. Nelson had been aware of all the activity around him and when he gave an account of the initial engagement he was quick to praise his friend:

> 'Captain Collingwood compelled the *San Ysidro* to hoist English colours and I thought the large ship *Salvador del Mundi* had also struck. But Collingwood disdaining the parade of taking possession of beaten enemies most gallantly pushed up with every sail set to save his old friend and messmate, who to all appearances, was in a critical state. The *Excellent* ranged up within ten feet of the *San Nicholas* 'giving her a most awful and tremendous fire.'

The impact of Collingwood's bombardment against the 'first-rate' *San Nicholas*, one of

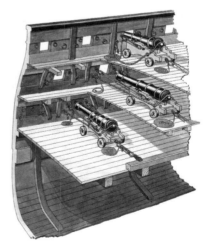

Three-tier gundecks on a man-o'-war

Spain's leading warship, had the effect of driving the vessel, or 'luffing' it, towards the *Captain*. The repeated broadsides had left the depleted Spanish crew demoralised and defeated. This event coincided with Nelson's capture of the *San Josef* and the commodore could not believe his luck when he found himself confronting the *San Nicholas* which had become entangled in the *San Josef's* rigging on the opposite starboard side. The three ships were quickly roped together and Nelson described how his crew boarded the second enemy vessel and very quickly overran it:

'The Spanish captain, with a bow, presented me with his sword and said the Admiral was dying of his wounds below. I asked him on his honour if the ship had surrendered. He declared she had, on which I gave him my hand and desired him to call his ship's company and tell them of it, which he did, and on the quarter deck of a Spanish first-rate, extravagant as the story may seem, did I receive the swords of the vanquished Spaniards, which as I received them, I gave to William Fearney one of my barge crew who put them, with sang-froid, under his arm.'

It was typical of Nelson's generosity to acknowledge the fearlessness of the ordinary seamen and to allow them to share in the glory. The success of the thirty-nine-year-old officer on 14th February added to the legend. Nelson enjoyed hearing that his achievement of capturing an enemy ship from the decks of another enemy ship, had been referred to as 'Nelson's Patent Bridge for boarding first-raters'.

It was an extraordinary sight to see the smallest vessel, *Captain*, rudderless, shot to pieces, yet attached to it were two mighty enemy ships displaying the English flags. But what was the reaction of his Commander-in-Chief to Nelson's 'disobedience'? Shortly after the battle, Nelson was sent for and he was relieved to be welcomed with open arms by Jervis and according to Nelson, the Admiral 'used every kind expression which could not fail to make me happy.' Not everyone rejoiced; there was an element of envy and jealousy within the ranks. Captain Calder hinted that the spontaneous manoeuvre, which carried Nelson and Collingwood into the brunt of the battle, was an unauthorised departure by the Commodore from the prescribed mode of attack - in other words it was a serious act of disobedience. 'It was certainly so,' said Jervis but he replied pointedly 'and if ever you commit such a breach of your orders, I will forgive you also.'

The Commander-in-Chief mentioned in his despatch that 'everyone had fought their ships well' and although Collingwood was singled out for special commendation, in the eyes of the public, Nelson was the hero of the hour. Two prizes had fallen to Nelson and he could fairly claim to have had the lion's share

Admiral Jervis was given the title Earl St Vincent in honour of his fleet's victory

on St Valentine's Day - which he did! His boasts caused much ill feeling in the fleet although not with men such as Collingwood who supported him up to the hilt. He knew Nelson well enough to understand that his actions spoke as loud as his words and he was sympathetically amused by his friend's self-satisfaction.

Everyone acknowledged that Collingwood's firepower had been superb; his crew's skills were unsurpassed and their speed and efficiency were held up as a yardstick for success. The Royal Navy would later call its gunnery school at Portsmouth *HMS Excellent* in honour of Collingwood. This was satisfaction enough for Cuthbert and his accomplishments were admired and appreciated in his native Tyneside; the North East were fully aware that their local hero was playing a major part in the defence of his nation.

There was correspondence from Nelson the day after the battle when he acknowledged the *Excellent's* major contribution:

My dearest friend [it was usually Dear Col]

"A friend in need is a friend indeed." Was never more truly verified than by your most noble and gallant conduct yesterday in sparing the *Captain* from further loss; and I beg, both as a public officer and a friend, that you will accept my most sincere thanks. I have not failed, by letter to the Admiral, to represent the eminent services of the *Excellent*. Tell me how you are; what are your disasters?

Collingwood wrote back immediately:

My dear good friend

First let me congratulate you on the success of yesterday - on the brilliance it attached to the British Navy, and the humility it must cause its enemies - and then let me congratulate my dear Commodore on the distinguished part which he ever takes when the honour and interests of his country are at stake. It added very much to the satisfaction I felt in thumping the Spaniards, that I released you a little.

I am ever dear friend, affectionately yours,

C Collingwood.

The mutual affection of the two men was genuine for they had shared so much together. There were two more letters that Cuthbert Collingwood received at this time that he would keep and treasure. The first came from Captain Dacres, who, at a time when self-promotion was rife, generously wrote:

My dear Sir

I have just time to request you will accept my congratulations upon the immortal honour gained by the *Excellent* yesterday. The Admiral joins very sincerely in my ideas. God bless you, and may we all imitate you.

Yours ever sincerely

J W Dacres

The Admiral that Captain Dacres referred to was the Hon. William Waldegrave who added his thoughts:

My dear Collingwood,

Although Dacres has in a great degree expressed all I feel on the subject, yet I cannot resist the satisfaction of telling you myself, that nothing in my opinion could exceed the spirit and true officership which you so happily displayed yesterday. Both Admiral Jervis and Nelson join with me in this opinion; and nothing but ignorance can think otherwise. God bless you good friend; and may England long possess such men as yourself - it is saying everything for her glory.

Truly yours,

William Waldegrave

When Collingwood was told by his Commander-in-Chief that he was to receive a gold medal for his bravery in the battle he told Admiral Jervis, quite firmly, that he could not accept. It may have seemed an insult to his commander but Collingwood, true to his principles, explained that he still felt slighted after the conflict three years earlier under Admiral Howe. Following the 'Glorious First of June' he wrote:

'I believe I was improperly passed over; and to receive such a distinction now would be to acknowledge the propriety of that injustice.'

It was a bold statement but the kindly Jervis replied with magnanimity:

'That is precisely the answer I expected from you Captain Collingwood.'

The Admiral had indeed anticipated that Collingwood might make such a stand and he was instrumental in seeing that the Northumbrian received two gold medals with the following inscriptions:

Cuthbert Collingwood Esquire, Captain of H.M.S. 'Excellent' on the 14th February MDCCXCVII. The Spanish fleet defeated.

and

Cuthbert Collingwood Esquire, Captain of H.M.S. 'Barfleur' on the 1st June MDCCICIV. The French fleet defeated.

The medals were highly valued and only sea officers could wear these coveted awards. Collingwood was proud to receive the recognition and to put the past injustice behind him. This is evident in the letter he sent to Dr Carlyle, where he reflects on 'Admiral Howe's plagued letter' and adds:

'His Majesty has been graciously pleased to make me all the amends he can, by sending me the medal for victory of June with that of February last.'

We learn something of Collingwood's character in the same correspondence where he urges the doctor that the award of his medals 'be not generally known, as it has too much the appearance of trumpeting which I detest.'

Captain Collingwood age 49

ADMIRAL COLLINGWOOD:

Watching and Waiting

We always are ready, steady, boys, steady.

After the high excitement and drama of a battle at sea, Collingwood found himself on policing duty once more. Jervis, now named Earl of St Vincent to commemorate his success, sent the *Excellent* to Cadiz to keep an eye on the Spanish fleet. Watching the enemy's movements was a necessary but grindingly boring activity, particularly for an active captain. Yet the vast majority of Collingwood's wartime service was just that, watching and waiting. The inactivity was difficult for the commander but it was also hard on the crew who became impatient and sullen. Collingwood always insisted on daily gunnery drills but the tedium of practice created resentment when there was little opportunity for the men to put their skills to the test. The poet Milton's maxim 'They also serve who only stand and wait' was true, but of little comfort to the restless seamen. The enemy would rather have gone about their business unobserved and unchallenged but they knew that if they were to leave their safe haven the British navy would be out to destroy them. The Spanish fleet did however have the advantage of a harbour anchorage and their men had access to dry land and fresh supplies whereas Collingwood and his command had to sit on the open sea, in the blazing sun, in the faint hope that their foes would attempt to break cover. Cuthbert spent much of his spare time corresponding and reflecting on his predicament as in the letter to his father-in-law dated 18 April 1797:

> 'We are not content with having beaten Spain at sea, but have now blocked up the port and are parading under the walls of Cadiz. The Spaniards have thirty-two sail of great ships ready, or nearly so - enough to devour us, if they but knew how to carve. We have heard that their seamen were offered double pay if they would exert themselves against us, which they decline as a hopeless undertaking, and have refused to come to sea: but I think they must come, or Spain is lost as a maritime power.'

In the same month he wrote to Nelson, who had just been promoted to the rank of Rear-Admiral of the Blue. The appointment had been made by seniority, Horatio moved up a few rungs after the conflict on the 14th of February which was now known officially as the 'Battle of St Vincent'. Nelson was leaving the 'watchers' and Collingwood hoped they would be together again soon:

> 'I am satisfied you know in my heart, that there are none in the fleet, few in the world, that I meet with more pleasure than yourself.'

Cuthbert then discussed the war predicament and the news that fourteen Spanish officers were hanged by their own people as a result of the Valentine Day defeat: 'What a fine promotion it will make in the Spanish Navy!' Collingwood saw the folly of exterminating experienced seamen and considered how insecure the promoted fourteen would feel by stepping into these dead-mens' shoes.

> 'If the Spaniards were in a state to come out, I should be sorry you were going from us, but your going is the strongest indication that the Admiral is certain they cannot come soon, or he would not part with such a precious limb from his body.'

There was prophetic irony in Collingwood's remarks for Nelson was ordered to Tenerife in an attempt to capture a Spanish treasure ship and it was here that he lost his right arm. He had been hit in the right elbow by a musket ball and later in the bowels of his ship the lifeless arm was sawn off. Nelson's foolhardy attack on Tenerife had been a catastrophic failure - a new experience for him - and it left him very despondent. The attack resulted in the needless loss of 153 men, one of whom was buried at sea, sewn up in a hammock with his Rear-Admiral's unwanted arm. On the positive side he received his substantial St Vincent prize money and his amputation entitled him, as befitting his rank, to £1,000 a year disability pension. With this newly-found wealth Horatio bought Fanny a

Lord Nelson minus right arm and right eye c.1801

home near Ipswich where he recuperated and they spent a happy period of time together before Nelson returned to sea.

The success of the Royal Navy had unexpected repercussions, for in April 1797, when the main British fleet was in the Mediterranean, a mutiny broke out at home. The nation had heaped praise upon its naval leaders; the King and Parliament rewarded their achievements, but the ordinary seamen had been overlooked and they felt aggrieved. Their discontent surfaced when the crews, anchored at Spithead near the important naval base of Portsmouth, refused to put out to sea and went on strike. This was unprecedented action and came at a sensitive time when Britain could not afford to lose her supremacy of the oceans. The sailors were no longer prepared to put up with squalid conditions, particularly on the lower decks, which were frequently filthy, rat-infested and disease-ridden. The public at large was not aware of the appalling living quarters, but inexcusably, the Admiralty and the government were. The mutiny in 1797 arose from the sailors' intolerable situation and not from any revolutionary principles; the ordinary seaman had simply had enough.

Their pay was twenty-four shillings a lunar month [£1.20p today. 2005 value = £120] for able seaman and nineteen shillings [90p] for ordinary seamen. After deductions they were lucky to get ten shillings [50p] a month.

This was bad enough, but their entitlement was often two or three years in arrears on a long voyage and pay was only issued in full when a ship was finally paid off. Their money was always in tickets that could only be converted into cash at the commissioning port, which may not have been where the seamen ended up. The sick on board the ship, whether through disease or war wounds, received no pay at all. It is not difficult to appreciate the resentment in the Royal Navy when the men saw that in the merchant sector, pay was three times better. The Army, which had achieved nothing in the field of battle, offered recruits more than twice as much as the sea-going warriors.

Out at sea, the food was very poor with the ordinary sailors typically receiving inedible bone and gristle and fat, cheese was inhabited by long red worms and the hard-tack, or ship's biscuits, were full of weevils. At mealtimes there was the sound of tapping as seaman knocked out the beetles; others ate them for added nutrition. There was a black joke that asked 'Which would you eat, the small or the large beetle?' Answer: 'You would always pick the lesser of two weevils'. The water supply was stored overlong in unclean barrels and became rancid so that the only reliable victual was rum. The men received half a pint, served diluted, in two portions a day. Even these unsavoury rations were in short measure because two ounces in every pound [one eighth] went directly to the purser, or head steward. The official daily ration became 1lb of salt pork [half-kilogram] or 2lb of salt beef on alternative days with 1lb of ship's biscuits [still with weevils] and a gallon of beer. This was to be supplemented with 2 pints [litre] of pease, 3 pints of oatmeal, 8 oz [500 grams] butter and 1lb of cheese. This may seem a substantial ration but still the purser took his percentage. The men also received antiscorbutics [lemons or limes] as a remedy against scurvy but these were supplied by the captain - they were not issued by officialdom.

Leave was virtually non-existent, for once the men left their ships they were unlikely to return and deserters were hanged, no questions asked. Medication at sea was usually administered by some incompetent and brutal student of medicine whose lack of skill had made him unfit for practice ashore - typically a drunk with a grievance.

The mutineer's claims were remarkably moderate. They did not call for the end of hanging at the yardarms, floggings at the gratings, or even the boatswain's habit of driving the men by beating them with a rope end. All they asked was that punishment should be within His Majesty's Regulations and comply with the instructions to servicemen. It was not an unreasonable request but at time of their complaint the men were being treated with a severity that was beyond endurance. The two sailor delegates at Spithead wanted an end to arbitrary and excessive punishment by tyrannical officers; they also felt

A purser

there should be some system whereby complaints could be considered. The protesters were not malcontents but 'prime seamen' often senior petty officers or gunner's mates - responsible men with skills and trades. The dispute became a major crisis when the marines, the epitome of military discipline, decided to back the claims of the seamen. An Act was hurried through Parliament and the pay was immediately improved. A Royal Pardon was granted to all who had mutinied and Lord Howe, Commander-in-Chief of the British fleet, visited the ships at Spithead and persuaded the men to return to duty.

The mutiny was settled a month after its outbreak, although there was another 'sympathy' strike at Nore and Yarmouth. Here the rebels were violent and less well organised. Collingwood described them as a 'floating republic':

> 'The seamen, I am persuaded, would never have revolted if there had been good order: but consider, with such a fleet as we now have, how large a proportion of the crews are miscreants of every description, and capable of every crime: and when these people predominate, what evils may we dread from such a mass of mischief!'

It is true that the British sailor was made up of every nationality imaginable, and that as well as the reluctant impressed men, there was a large proportion of convicts - such was the shortage of manpower.

There was a suggestion that the influence of the much-despised French Revolution was infecting the navy and that Richard Parker, the ringleader in Nore, was a traitor. The ordinary loyal, law-abiding sailors, when they witnessed the peaceful settlement at Spithead, decided to get rid of Parker. They handed him over to the authorities and he was hanged along with 29 of his fellow prisoners after 59 had been charged.

The gallows at Tyburn where, in the late 1700s, ten victims could be hanged at the same time

Parker was suspended from the yardarm of his ship and a grandstand was erected on the shore so that spectators could witness the gruesome executions. The men who escaped hanging were either imprisoned or flogged and it is reported that some received up to 380 lashes. It is unlikely that this number was reached, for death would surely have come before a fraction of the strokes had been administered.

The former mutinous ships and their crews were redistributed within the Royal Navy and many of them came to Collingwood. The potentially disastrous situation had been resolved by the 'manly and generous character of British seaman' said William Pitt which was not how he had described them a month earlier. Proof that the men were loyal to their King and country came later in

October when Admiral Duncan's squadron of sixteen, took on the Dutch Fleet and the British seamen captured eleven enemy ships.

Collingwood hated the idea of mutiny as vehemently as he hated revolution. He was a believer in discipline but he was very fair and his men recognised this. The Northumbrian cared about his crew and supported these simple, often illiterate men who were devoted to the King in a way which would seem incomprehensible today. They were tough and uncomplaining and only sought consideration, justice and leadership to prove themselves the best sailors afloat. If anyone on board Cuthbert Collingwood's ship described a member of the crew as acting in a mutinous way he reacted strongly. He would declare:

'Mutiny? If mutiny could have arrived in my ship then it would be my fault and every one of the officers. It is a charge of the gravest nature.'

If there were ungovernable spirits in the British fleet the usual response was 'Send them to Collingwood.' The kind but firm conduct that he adopted towards his men enabled him to maintain discipline without the necessity of bringing men to trial for their lives; hanging was a commonplace event that Collingwood despised. A seaman from the *Rombus* was sent to the *Excellent* after he had turned a cannon on the officers and threatened to fire at them unless he received a promise that he would not be punished. On the *Excellent*, in front of many sailors, Collingwood was reported as addressing the new arrival with the words:

'I know your character well, but beware how you attempt to excite subordination in this ship; for I have such confidence in my men, that I am certain I shall hear in an hour of anything you are doing. If you behave well in the future, I will treat you like the rest, nor notice here what happened in another ship; but if you endeavour to excite mutiny, mark me well, I will instantly head you up in a cask, and throw you into the sea.'

The man evidently became a good and obedient sailor and never again gave cause for complaint.

On those occasions when Collingwood was obliged to use corporal punishment, and they were rarer than most, he had to be present as it was customary to read the Articles of War [the rule book] and it was said that he suffered wounded feelings just as much as the culprit himself. Witnesses reported that their leader was for many hours melancholy and silent, sometimes not speaking a word for the remainder of the day.

Nelson, however, felt no such compunction, and in that respect he was more a man of the times. In his ship's punishment book, between the end of July 1803 (when the Victory had joined the fleet in the Gulf of Lions) and December 1804 there were 380 entries related to the infliction of the lash - an average of six each week. In one period alone, from January to July 1804, 105 men were flogged, thirteen of them more than once. An outstanding case was that of John Walsh who was punished four times; for theft (12 lashes) 10th January; drunkenness (36 lashes) 24th March; more drunkenness (48 lashes) 5th April; more theft (48 lashes) 24th May - and physical punishment was supposed to be a deterrent! There were instances of 'flogging round the fleet' and this brutal

51

measure was inflicted on Richard Collins, William Brown and John Marshall. They were condemned to receive 200 lashes each, 50 alongside the Victory and 50 alongside three other ships. Their crime was desertion - presumably whilst on a watering party abroad - and desertion was usually punishable by hanging. Whether Nelson's cat-o'-nine-tails alternative was more merciful is open to doubt - it is unlikely that their bodies could have survived the shock of 200 consecutive lashes. The apparently sadistic public performance was carried out as a fearful reminder to men who may have considered jumping ship. Floggings were a ritualistic spectacle which were witnessed by the entire crew. It took up a considerable amount of time to rig the gratings, strip the victims, read the 'articles' and administer the beatings. In the teeming, defenceless world of shipboard life there was little sympathy for the culprits and the regularity of floggings became a matter of indifference to the observers. The most frequent crimes were - fighting, uncleanness, insolence, contempt, theft, drunkenness, and disobedience.

Thomas Hardy, Nelson's flag-captain, was said to be a harsh, bullying commander. Hardy shared a close bond of friendship with Horatio although physically it was an unequal match; The flag-captain was six-feet-four-inches tall - colossal for a Georgian seaman - and Nelson was very slightly-built. Paintings of

A public flogging on board ship

death scenes in the *Victory* have always reduced Hardy and raised the admiral so that their heights were artistically compatible. On the quarterdeck there is evidence to suggest that Admiral Nelson would have supported his flag-captain's attitude towards punishment. As a general rule he left the discipline, and running of the ship, to his subordinates although he must bear some responsibility for condoning his captain's fondness for the lash.

By contrast, Collingwood, as a captain, punished when he felt compelled to do so. As an admiral he discouraged flogging, and saw to it that his captains acted as he wished. It was not Collingwood's way to stand back and let the captain and officers control the ship. It was said that he referred to senior officers as 'assistants', as if he personally ran the ship, which of course he did. It was a time when the wretched pressed men had their sufferings multiplied and captains like Thomas Hardy felt they had to brutalise men into obedience and submission for the sake of good discipline. The poet John Masefield was moved to write that 'our naval glory was built up by the blood and agony of thousands of barbarously maltreated men.' Not on Cuthbert Collingwood's ship. His abhorrence of corporal punishment increased as he grew older. When Collingwood became Commander-in-Chief in the Mediterranean many years later he refused to allow a ship to join his fleet because of the notoriety of its regime:

> 'I expect no good service from her, and her example may be pernicious. In her present state I feel she should be removed to England; for even without a ship in her stead, I shall consider the squadron as much strengthened by her being withdrawn from it.'

At this time there were two well-publicised court-martials where able seamen were on trial for disobeying orders and they were, unusually for the times, acquitted. The release was justified as it was proved that 'great severity was the reason for their adverse reaction.' The younger captains had beaten the men into a state of insubordination. Collingwood remarked:

> 'The only defence for the brutality was that of youth and inexperience, yet it is this very same youth and inexperience that our country is entrusted to.'

Nevertheless, he was determined that his men should respect authority and when a young midshipman made a complaint, he felt obliged to uphold the punishment handed out by these young burgeoning officers and would order the punishment to take place the following day. He would then call the midshipman to him and say:

> 'In all probability the fault is yours, but whether it was or not, I am sure it would pain your heart to see a man, old enough to be your father, disgraced and punished on your account; and it will, therefore, give me a good opinion of you if, when he is brought out, you ask for his pardon.'

When this recommendation (effectively an order) was carried out, the lad would intercede for the prisoner and Collingwood would make a great play of refusing to yield but at length would say to the guilty seaman:

> 'This young gentleman has pleaded so humanely for you, that I hope that you will feel a due gratitude to him and I will for the time being overlook your offence.'

Alternative punishment which Collingwood found to have a better outcome, was to exclude a seaman from his mess. Keeping the offender away from his mates was a miserable punishment on a small craft, especially as he would be ostracised by his peers. Most sailors preferred the short, sharp cat-o'-nine tails to being in disgrace and ignored.

Another effective punishment was to water the grog. All the men received a half a pint of rum a day and this came in two quarter pint measures. Each quarter pint and was topped up with three times as much water and these two pint portions of grog were served up during each working day. The grog produced mild inebriation but to water it down even further was to remove the intoxicating effect and this was seen as real punishment. The men seemed to function better under a haze of alcohol and it was standard practice to issue an extra ration of grog before a battle. The men saw this as an anticipatory reward for a forthcoming encounter but in fact it was more likely given to raise the aggressive levels amongst the men and to take the edge off their fear.

Recklessness and bravado - even if fuelled by rum - was encouraged.

Collingwood demonstrated care and concern for his crew without any outward show. He visited his men daily when they were sick and gave them food from his table. The sailors called him 'father' and when they changed ships, many men were seen in tears at their departure. But he was not a man who courted popularity. He disliked bad manners and he would tell his officers 'if you do not know a man's name, then call him 'sailor' and not 'you sir!' If he had cause to rebuke or reprimand his crew, his words would be short and sharp, and always conveyed in the language of a gentleman. Chastisements were deeply felt, particularly by the youngsters in his care. Captain Collingwood treated midshipmen with parental concern and each week he made a point of testing them on their learning. He was very much in the stern schoolteacher mould and perhaps his old headmaster, the Rev Hugh Moises, was his model. Collingwood instructed the boys in the essential details of the service and he expected his pupils to acquire a habit of discipline, punctuality, cleanliness, diligence and the Georgian virtues of sobriety and self-denial. He believed in the naval adage that 'learning to *obey*, teaches how to *command*.' Many boys passed the compulsory lieutenant's examination under his instruction and that led them on the path to becoming officers. Collingwood invested a great deal of care in his charges and he admitted that :

'Nothing gives me greater pain than a boy who has failed to pass.'

It was a restless time for Britain because they could see the French military dominating the continent and they were powerless to stop them. They learnt that a Lieutenant Bonaparte had quelled a 1795 riot in Paris by firing a 'whiff of grapeshot' into the crowds. This same soldier, now a general, had led a brilliant 1796-7 Italian campaign. His success was so impressive that the Directory of Paris, the ruling authority, offered Napoleon the choice of two possible campaigns, a) invading Britain or b) conquering Egypt. He chose the latter. After Egypt he would turn his attention to Britain - with a vengeance! Napoleon's plans were, in his own words:

'To go to Egypt, to establish myself there and found a French Colony, will require some months. But as soon as I have made England tremble for the safety of India, I shall return to Paris, and give the enemy its deathblow. There is nothing to fear in the interval. Europe is calm. Austria cannot attack. England is occupied with preparing her defences against invasion and we can expect an uninterrupted journey.'

General Bonaparte, at twenty-nine years of age, was supremely confident and not without reason for it seemed that at present Great Britain was abandoning the Mediterranean to concentrate its fleet in the home waters

Napoleon Bonaparte

54

were it was believed a French attack was imminent. Napoleon Bonaparte landed at Egypt with 30,000 infantry, 2,800 cavalry and 100 field and siege guns from 300 transport ships. Thirteen ship-of-the-line warships and seven frigates accompanied this huge convey yet Nelson, who was sent with a 15-ship squadron to intercept the enemy, had missed them.

It was on the 1st of August 1798 by the time Nelson eventually caught up with the French fleet. They were anchored in Aboukir Bay by the mouth of the River Nile and the troops had disembarked several weeks earlier. This did not deter Nelson as he decided to attack the fleet where they were situated in spite of their strong defensive position. He employed two unusual tactics; firstly he began the battle as it was becoming dark, and secondly he attacked the French ships by coming between the enemy and the shore in dangerously shallow water. The unexpected approach took Admiral Brueys by surprise and allowed Nelson to take the initiative. Brueys was leading the defence from aboard the *L'Orient*, a colossal 120-gun, three-decker ship that was taking a tremendous pounding from the more manoeuvrable British vessels. The French defensive lines had gaps between them and this suited the smaller craft that could get amongst the enemy ships and 'rake' them. Raking was a merciless tactic as it involved firing through the length of a ship from the vulnerable stern through to the bow. The ship's guns, situated on both sides, were powerless to prevent the devastating effect of raking which ripped through the decks, sweeping away men and their cannons.

Admiral Brueys

The British fleet were successfully eliminating the opposition and gradually their attention was directed towards *L'Orient*, the flagship, which was now aflame. All available ships fired relentlessly into her, determined to make the Admiral lower her tricolour flag and surrender. An eyewitness account from John Lee of the *Swiftsure* told of the dogged French determination:

'The brave Brueys having lost both his legs, was seated with tourniquets on the stumps in an armchair facing his enemies, and giving directions for extinguishing the fire, when a cannon-ball from our ship put a period to his gallant life by nearly cutting him in two.'

Men began jumping from the doomed ship and the young son of the fated Captain Casabianca was seen, standing helpless and wounded. This scene was the inspiration for the melodramatic poem 'The Boy stood on the Burning Deck.' A few moments later *L'Orient* exploded with devastating effect and the sound could be heard fifteen miles away. This effectively ended the battle and it was a major victory for Nelson who confiscated, burnt, or sank the nine ships in his possession - although four French vessels escaped. The magnificent *L'Orient*, sank to the bottom with half a million pounds in gold bullion, three tons of plate, the treasures of the Knights of Malta and the money that Napoleon had brought with him to finance the Egyptian campaign. The Battle of the Nile, as it became known, had stranded Napoleon and his troops in Egypt and Nelson ordered a watch to be placed upon the coastline to prevent the General from returning to France by sea. This was a serious reversal for Napoleon; France was not accustomed to losing battles.

The explosion of the French flagship L'Orient

The immediate threat to the English coastal waters was nullified once more. Collingwood was not involved in the battle although nothing would have given him greater pleasure than to have fought the old enemy. Horatio Nelson's triumph added to his fame and there was widespread hero–worship for the wiry leader. His crew loved him for the success he had achieved because it rubbed off onto the lowliest seaman. It was not just his men who idolised him; a certain Lady Emma Hamilton also took to the streets of Naples to lead a victory parade in his honour. Nelson brought his *Vanguard* into Naples for repairs and Lady H. prepared a grand ball to celebrate both his success and his 40th birthday. Emma flattered Horatio and he revelled in the attention; the fact that he was a married man made no difference to her attentions.

Collingwood was generous in his praise for Nelson and he never once criticised his friend. After the Battle of the Nile he wrote:

'Nelson is an incomparable man, without much previous preparation of plan, he has the faculty of discovering advantages as they arise and good judgement to turn them to his use. An enemy that commits a false step is ruined.'

Cuthbert had hoped to be alongside Nelson but his ship the *Excellent* was long overdue to return to England and Lord St Vincent felt that Collingwood was too valuable a member of his fleet to risk as well as Nelson. His seniority should have ensured that he joined Horatio, but although he privately felt aggrieved, he refused to show it and praised his friend:

'It was the promptitude, as much as the vigour of the attack, which gave Nelson the superiority so very soon. The Frenchman found himself assailed before he had determined how best to repel the assault, and when victory had been decided on our side the fruits of it were carefully gathered in.'

By the end of the year Collingwood could not wait to return home. It was an enormous relief for the Tyneside captain to be allowed shore leave from his long arduous tour of duty and he arrived in Spithead in December 1798. He was offered the command of the 90-gun *Atlas* that was ready to sail but he had no hesitation in turning it down. To be on English soil once again lifted his spirits although it took weeks to eventually pay off his crew, complete his reports and finally vacate his ship. Collingwood left behind the *Excellent*, a ship that he had immortalised. His ability to fire three broadsides in a phenomenal two-and-a-half minutes became legendary. By the end of January 1799 Collingwood finally headed for Northumberland. It was four years since he had seen his wife Sarah and his young daughters and he was savouring the moment:

'To be let loose to the greatest enjoyment a human creature is capable of, the sweet caress of a beloved wife and children (for I expect they will make much of me) and the affection and regard of a family and friends that are very dear to me.'

The dull days at sea were behind him, he was carefree and relaxed; he had earned his rest.

The River Wansbeck, Morpeth, Collingwood's house is the tallest in the picture

During this period ashore he learned that he had been promoted to Rear-Admiral of the White, at the age of fifty. The appointment was dated 14 February 1799 exactly two years after the St Vincent battle. Cuthbert Collingwood had served the King for thirty-eight years and there would be few in the navy, including Nelson, who could match his continuous employment.

The City of Newcastle wined and dined their hero and Collingwood was 'flattered by their kind reception' and admitted that 'I have scarce sat half an hour at a time, except at a feast.' He was gracious and appreciative of the attention but after a while Collingwood began to feel the weight of his naval responsibility. The promotion highlighted his important position in the fleet and it reminded him that the nation was living through a menacing period. Admirals were often removed from active service and given shore-based employment and this was something that Cuthbert would have to consider. He confided in Dr Carlyle once again:

'I have spent a month in great happiness. Every body and every object contributes to it. My Sarah is all that is excellent in a woman, my two girls are sweet creatures and appear to have the greatest affection for their mother and for each other, and they seem to possess tempers that promise them a fair share of happiness. So, if this great promotion which the King has made in the Navy should exclude me from serving at sea.. then I have as many comforts, and sources of normal happiness, to resort to as any other person. But I shall never lose sight of the duty I owe to my country.'

For Collingwood, King and country was always the first priority.

By March, Collingwood was back in London at the Admiralty offering his services:

'I have health and strength in me at present for anything. Our operations at sea are those of most consequence to the defence of our country. I am sick with abhorrence of the French; every year they grow in strength and it is difficult to see how, or when, their tyranny will end. I cannot in the present state of things, suppress an impatience to be in the exercise of my profession.'

He was home again during the whole of April but in May he was summoned to serve in the channel fleet under Lord Bridport. Collingwood was grateful for his wife's understanding, as he explained to Dr Carlyle:

'Sarah misses me but does not make my absence more painful by complaint. She accepts that when my country needs my service, I am devoted to it.'

The appointment to his allotted ship was not to his satisfaction. After his previous vessel, according to the new Rear-Admiral, the 35-year-old *Triumph* was inappropriately named:

'She is a bad sailer. She sails so very ill - much worse than the *Excellent*, on her worst day. If the fleet were not to stop for me a little, I should be left.'

It must have been galling for Collingwood, who was regarded by his peers as having unrivalled sailing skills. It was frustrating to be in command of a sluggish two-decker but another disappointment for Collingwood was that he felt that his captain was not up to the job. The Rear-Admiral took the major decisions on board the *Triumph* but it was generally accepted that a captain was responsible for the handling of the ship and its crew. To have an admiral who demanded the highest of standards alongside him on the quarterdeck would have been extremely daunting for any captain.

Collingwood's increased status did have a drawback as he was now subordinate to fellow admirals in the fleet and had to follow their instructions. It must have taken a great deal of self-control to carry out actions that went against the grain. Collingwood, like Nelson, was a fighter who never shirked a confrontation and he clearly felt that his

Rear-Admiral Collingwood

superiors in the fleet were too cautious and hesitant. This was difficult enough for Collingwood but he also believed that the leaders were not sufficiently vigilant. The reason for the British fleet's existence was to blockade the ports and prevent French ships from leaving. Their dual role was also to stop enemy ships from arriving at the ports to strengthen their existing flotilla. At this time, the French fleet were under the command of the wily Admiral Bruix and he seemed to have a wandering brief as he roamed around the European coastline creating havoc. The British were anxious that Bruix did not team up with the Spanish fleet for that would have doubled their strength. It seems from Cuthbert's perspective that the home fleet under Lord St Vincent and Lord Keith were chasing the tail of the French and were never quite able to pin down the enemy admiral to confront him. Bruix was a source of constant irritation as he interfered with convoys, attacked the British possessions and overwhelmed isolated naval detachments. Rear-Admiral Collingwood was the master of his trade and he found it very frustrating watching the antics of seniors who seemed to be pre-occupied with their petty squabbles whilst France 'led them a dance.' Cuthbert had too much time to think and little chance to act; it was a long weary period for the Tynesider.

Finally the British pursuers caught up with the enemy at Brest and this was their opportunity. Collingwood wrote to his sister with the brackets '(between ourselves)' then explained how the cornered French slipped through their fingers:

'The French fleet came out at last when the weather was thick and hazy but Captain Percy lost sight of them. He took it into his head (which I imagine is something like the weather) that they had gone into port again.'

Collingwood implied that the inside of Percy's head was thick and hazy, then he caustically posed the question:

'Would the French have come out just to show how well they could go in again?'

When the mist cleared, the British entered the port of Brest and found they had gone. The months of constant surveillance had ended in failure. Collingwood felt bitter humiliation and although he did not openly criticise his seniors by name, his frustration at a lost opportunity for conflict with the French, was apparent in a letter to his Uncle, Sir Edward Blackett, dated 17 August 1799:

'It was horrible bungling work. I am afraid we shall be very unwelcome to England, returning from so fair a field for great deeds, having effected nothing. The fleets of France and Spain seemed to be in our path, there was an opportunity at least to combat them, and we had a force that promised everything, but the truth is, our efforts were not great. I do not pretend to give reasons why they were not - the way of the escaping fleet was obvious to everyone, but we did not go that way. To those of us in the fleet who looked to the country's best interest, and whose only object was the destruction of the enemy's fleet, it has been a continuous series of vexations and disappointments. We have made a most unfortunate voyage of it.'

What Collingwood did not know, was that the blockade at Aboukir Bay, the scene of Nelson's victorious Battle of the Nile, was equally unsuccessful. A day after Collingwood's letter, two French frigates sailed out of the River Nile under cover of darkness and one of them was carrying Napoleon Bonaparte back to France, right under the noses of the British commander, Sir Sidney Smith and his squadron. It was more horrible, bungling work. The French general had abandoned his troops in Egypt to make a dash for it and he was not stopped. He received a hero's welcome when he reached French soil and with this popular support he swept aside the outworn, ruling Directory. Bonaparte then proceeded to re-write the constitution and elected himself First Consul and ultimately he appointed himself Emperor - a far cry from republican democracy. In a few short weeks Napoleon had leapt from being a fugitive in a frigate to the elevated seat of power. If Smith had been more vigilant, he could have prevented the rise of the 'Little General' and perhaps the subsequent fifteen years of terrible war and bloodshed could have been avoided.

By the end of October, Rear-Admiral Collingwood was in brighter spirits and in his letter to his sister Mary he describes how Captain Digby of his fleet had captured a Spanish frigate which had 1,411,500 dollars on board. Although nowhere near the scene of action, Collingwood's seniority entitled him to a share of the sum that converted to £80,000. His entitlement was £2,000 [2005 = £200,000] and he described this as a 'no bad Michaelmas goose.' Dr Carlyle congratulated him on his windfall but typically Collingwood was dismissive:

'It's a comfortable thing to be at ease in pecuniary matters but I do not consider it as a thing that has any relation to our [marital] happiness, and I believe Sarah feels very much as I do on the subject. I do like to hear my wife praised and your sentiments of her brought a pleasure to my heart that prizes never did.'

As the new millennium arrived, Collingwood was reflecting on the prospect of peace and his homecoming. His thoughts drifted to his Morpeth garden where his cares could be forgotten:

'I will plant my cabbages again, and prune my gooseberry bushes, cultivate roses, and twist the woodbine through the hawthorn with as much satisfaction as ever Dioclesian had, and with the same desire and hope that the occasion never will recur to call me back to more important but less pleasurable occupations.'

Cuthbert's classical education had brought to mind the Roman

Collingwood House 1936

emperor, Dioclesian, who had ruled for twenty-one years before retiring to the olive groves of his native Dalmatia.

The Rear-Admiral was unusual in the fleet for he had plants on board his ship which he nurtured and cared for. He would write:

'This is the third summer that I have hardly seen the leaf of the trees, except through a glass at a distance of some leagues.'

It was very frustrating to be sailing near home waters and yet to be effectively separated from his loved ones by the length of England. Perhaps it was this inaccessibility that led to letters of uncharacteristic despondency:

'I feel a sadness and depression of spirits. The only time I am free of this oppressive something, as if I bore a mountain on my shoulders, is the first four hours that I am dispatching my business, and at the time I know no ill, all is brisk with me.'

At other times he wrote of a 'dreadful languor which I cannot shake off' but then he described how once retired he would be cured:

'I should prescribe a cheerful friend or two, who could be merry without being loud, light and nourishing food and a bottle (at least) of good claret after dinner.'

In early 1801, Cuthbert was ashore in Portsmouth, and although he could not be released to travel north, his wife and daughter were making the arduous 400-mile trip from Northumberland to visit him. Sarah was arranging to buy the substantial family house in Morpeth that they were at present renting. Collingwood was unable to assist with the transaction and his father-in-law who was living with Sarah, was becoming quite elderly. John Erasmus Blackett had been Mayor of Newcastle on several occasions but he was becoming extremely deaf and needed looking after. In spite of the domestic upheaval, Sarah and 'Sall', now aged eight, left their home in the middle of winter, to travel south in a horse-drawn carriage. The journey would have lasted at least two weeks on difficult roads in unpredictable weather and limited daylight. Collingwood was delighted that his family would be with him, although his youngest daughter Mary Patience, was thought to be too young to travel, even though there was only twelve month's difference between the ages of the girls. As Collingwood anxiously awaited their arrival he received a visit from his closest friend, Horatio Nelson.

Horatio had only been on British soil for two months following a triumphal return from Palermo in Sicily. He was ordered back to England but was informed that his flagship was needed in the Mediterranean so he had to make an overland journey home. By a happy coincidence (for Horatio) Sir William, whose health was failing, was replaced by another ambassador and the Hamiltons were also asked to return to England which allowed Nelson to travel back with Emma and her husband. The entourage came home via Vienna, Prague, Dresden and other German cities. Wherever they went, Emma and Nelson were treated like celebrities and grand balls and feasts were held in their honour. Nelson, after all, was the only man in Europe to have stopped Napoleon in his tracks and he had effectively thwarted the general's plans in Egypt. Horatio had also stood by King Ferdinand of Naples and his queen Maria. He offered the ships of the Royal Navy for their protection and gave them refuge when the monarchy was driven out of Naples by the French. Nelson helped restore Ferdinand to the throne and was instrumental in publicly executing the king's Neapolitan rebels. For his service to the king he was given the Dukedom of Bronte, an area on the slopes of Mount Etna. Nelson was so delighted to acquire the land and farms, which yielded an income of £3,000 a year, that from that day forward he always signed his name 'Nelson Bronte'.

By the time the party reached England, word was out that the hero of the Nile was consorting with Sir William Hamilton's wife and the satirical cartoonists of the day sharpened their quill pens. The scurrilous press reached new levels of cruelty as they depicted Emma Hamilton as gross, overweight and behaving like a spoilt child. Nelson was portrayed as a diminutive, gullible suitor overwhelmed by the power of this grasping woman. This was the media.

Lady Hamilton, as lampooned by the press

However, the common folk loved Horatio and when he arrived at Great Yarmouth, thousands turned out to catch a glimpse of Norfolk's forty-two-year-old national icon. The people idolised him; he had made their lives safe by his brilliant acts of bravery. Nelson enjoyed the adulation and was happy to exchange banter with the crowds. A landlady wanted to change the name of her inn to the 'Nelson's Arms' and he joked 'But I only have one arm.'

After the jubilant welcome he finally met up with his wife Fanny. It had been three years since he had last seen her and she knew all the gossip. It was evident that in the long absence a wide gulf had developed, physically and emotionally. Fanny expected her husband to remain at her side but his thoughts were elsewhere. She confronted Horatio with the words 'I am resolved that you give up either her or me.' Nelson made his choice and left his wife. He allowed Fanny to live in his London home; made arrangements for her to receive a generous quarterly allowance, then declared: 'I never mean to see her again.' The lovesick admiral was drawn to Lady Hamilton and what the public did not know, was that Emma was in the final few days of pregnancy. Nelson felt that he should not be seen too close to Emma at this sensitive period when the press were at their most unforgiving. He was in desperate need of a sympathetic companion, so he turned to Cuthbert Collingwood.

Cuthbert remained a true, loyal friend to Horatio at the time of his separation from Fanny. Nelson knew that in Collingwood he had a discreet confidant who would not pass judgment upon him. Horatio had confided in his friend for many years and it would seem that he was happy to move in with Cuthbert. That is the impression that Collingwood conveys in a letter to his father-in-law in a letter dated January the 25th 1801:

'Lord Nelson is here, and I think he will probably come and live with me when the weather will allow him. He gave me an account of his reception at Court, which was not very flattering, after having been the admiration of Naples. His Majesty merely asked him if he had recovered his health, and then without waiting for an answer, turned to General _____ [unnamed] and talked to him near half an hour in great good humour.'

Collingwood seems to have been affronted that the king should have ignored the naval representative in favour of the army for he added:

'The king could not have talked to the general about <u>his</u> successes.'

There had not been any!

Nelson's very public affair was frowned upon but there was also the fact that the clergyman's son was getting above himself. Nelson had accepted a Dukedom from a minor foreign monarch and was flaunting his newfound status in public. The establishment felt Horatio needed bringing down a peg or two. So, shunned by the Court and ridiculed by the press, Nelson felt isolated and ostracised. His one great comfort was reliable old Collingwood. Their lives had run a parallel course and they had shared so many experiences. They would converse for hours on personal and naval issues; they were soul mates and their bond of mutual respect was unbreakable.

Whilst the friends dined, Collingwood received a message from the nearby Fountains Inn to say his wife and daughter had arrived safely after their long overland journey from Northumberland. Cuthbert excused himself:

'I flew to the inn where I had desired my wife to come, and I found her and little Sarah as well after their journey as if it had lasted only for a day. Human nature is not capable of a greater happiness that was mine that evening; but at dawn we parted, and I went to sea.'

Collingwood's sense of duty was uppermost. He is not bemoaning the fact that the he is leaving his loved ones, rather he seems to be grateful that the navy allowed him time off, even if it was fleeting. He adds that:

'Lord St Vincent has, however, been so good as to promise that I shall go to Plymouth whenever I can be spared from the fleet.'

The reunion at the inn was a joyful occasion for Cuthbert as he was surrounded by those he loved most - even his best friend was not excluded. Nelson accepted the invitation to join the family gathering and he spent a delightful evening with the Collingwoods. Cuthbert later described the scene to Mrs Moutray, his friend from the Antiguan days whom he still kept in touch with:

'How surprised you would have been, to have popped into the Fountains

Inn, and seen Lord Nelson, my wife, and myself sitting cosily by the fireside, watching little Sarah teaching Phillis, her dog, to dance.'

Nelson liked Collingwood's wife and daughter very much and the evening they spent together was a poignant reminder of a warm, family life. At this time, Emma would have been at the forefront of Nelson's thoughts for a week after this event, he became the father of a daughter, Horatia. Their illegitimate child was a well-kept secret and it was not until two years later, after Sir William Hamilton had died, that they set up home together. Nelson used up almost all of his savings to buy Merton Place, a palatial country retreat where they lived with Horatia. They could not marry but at a special ceremony just before Trafalgar they exchanged gold rings to seal their 'pure and innocent friendship'. It was at Merton Place with Emma and his daughter that Nelson experienced the domestic bliss that he craved for.

Collingwood also desired domesticity and whilst his family remained close at hand, they were very much out of reach. Sarah meanwhile, found a lodging house in Plymouth, where everyone was very attentive to her needs. She was surprised by the cold weather which seemed to penetrate her bones. Three weeks after arriving she wrote to her uncle, Sir Edward Blackett:

'The weather here is very severe, I have been confined to the house some days with rheumatism, but hope to get out again soon. I wish I could give you an account of Admiral Collingwood but he is kept at sea. In the meantime, I have the satisfaction of knowing how much my husband is respected here by the very great kindness and attention that everybody shows me. I might, if I pleased, be engaged out every day; but as I have my little girl with me, that would not answer at all, as it would be leaving her too much, so I shall now stay more at home.'

It must have been frustrating for Cuthbert to have been patrolling at Ushant, so close to the shore, but circumstances kept him at sea as he explained to his father-in-law:

'I have little chance of seeing her again, unless a storm should drive us into port, for the French fleet is in a state of preparation and we have to watch them narrowly.'

Another frustration was that Collingwood had not received newspapers or letters from England nor did his own correspondence seem to be getting through. Normally the communication in home waters was a priority but for the past three weeks when Cuthbert was anxious for his waiting family he admitted:

'We are immured within the sides of our ships, and have no knowledge of the world or its ways.'

Soon after, he was allowed four days with his wife and daughter. He even took them out to sea but this was not a happy experience:

'They came aboard the *Barfleur* at Cawsand and unluckily a hard gale of wind came on which made them very ill and not a little glad to get on shore again as soon as the storm abated. I will not prevail upon them to come aboard again.'

Sarah had been given a harsh insight into how her husband was employed. Back on dry land she took her daughter to stay at Paignton; 'a very pleasant village near Torquay' is how Collingwood described it. He had hoped that 'some good gale might drive us in there' but that did not happen. Collingwood sent a note to his wife, dated 24th August, requesting her to return to Plymouth as he expected a brief shore leave. He spent time with his Sarah's during September and October which meant that for the ten-month stay Collingwood had only been with them for barely three weeks. On Collingwood's final day ashore, he was preparing to go to sea, when his servant William brought news to his room. He described the scene to his father-in-law:

> 'He came running in with one of his important faces on, and attempted to give his information in a speech; but after two or three efforts, which were a confused huddle of inarticulate sounds, he managed to bring out, Peace! Peace! Which had just as good effect as the finest oration he could have made on the subject.'

During this period when Collingwood was on local patrol, Nelson had been in action doing what he did best. Sir Hyde Parker, with Nelson as second in command, led the British fleet into a conflict that became known as the Battle of Copenhagen. Denmark had been forced into an alliance with the French and as a consequence became the enemy of King George. The great fear was that if the Danish ships joined up with the enemy fleet then that would increase the threat to the Royal Navy. In a repeat performance of the Battle of the Nile, Nelson took on the anchored Danes in shallow water and Britain proved her superiority once more. But it was a fearsome struggle and Sir Hyde Parker was convinced his fleet were taking a beating and he signalled with flags to 'break off the action'. Nelson, who was in the thick of it, literally saw things differently, for he famously said to his men:

> 'I only have one eye, I have a right to be blind sometimes.'

He then put his telescope up to his blind right eye and declared 'I really don't see the signal' and he carried on fighting and achieved the victory.

It had been a very bloody encounter; the British lost 1,000 men and three captains, as neither side would yield until the bitter end. The Danes refused to surrender until an exasperated Nelson told them to cease firing at once otherwise he would burn all the ships he had captured. A

Battle of Copenhagen

truce was immediately arranged. The next day Nelson went ashore and over the following week negotiated a settlement. Sir Hyde Parker was ordered to hand over the command to his number two and he returned to England in disgrace where he was vilified for his timidity. Nelson's victory brought the Russians and the Swedes into line and nullified the potential danger in the Baltic.

It had been another success for Nelson but on this occasion there were few cheers. Britain had always been on good terms with Denmark but the hateful French had forced their traditional allies into a reluctant battle. The Royal Navy admired the Danes and there was no satisfaction in the killing of friends. Nelson saw things differently and he believed that the action was undervalued and did a great disservice to the 'brave fellows' who had died. Nelson tried to persuade the Admiralty that gold medals ought to have been struck but his request did not meet with approval. What the battle did reinforce, was the continued supremacy of the Royal Navy and this no doubt contributed to the peace treaty that Collingwood alluded to. If good can come from war, then it has to be said that this terrible conflict hastened the Treaty of Amiens which was signed on the 25th May 1802. This agreement committed the signatories to a lasting peace.

On Friday 7th May the Northumbrian made, what he assumed would be the final entry in his maritime journal, when he lowered his Rear-Admiral flag and wrote 'At sunset I struck my flag by order.' It must have been quite a poignant moment for Collingwood. He was approaching his 54th birthday, which was a very advanced age in the early 19th century, and at long last it seemed that he would be able to spend his days at home. On the long journey back to Morpeth, to his wife, to his children, to his garden, he must have felt a joyous sense of anticipation.

The British fleet

REAR-ADMIRAL COLLINGWOOD
Peace and War

For who are so free as the sons of the waves?

Collingwood had barely settled in when he was writing letters once again. This time it was to his sister-in-law, encouraging her to leave the South to sample the virtues of the North:

'I would recommend Northumberland for your residence. It has a fine healthy air throughout the year; in winter, a comfortable fire and friends about you that would be made happy by your company. Here we are a set of happy creatures. The bathing at Newbiggin has given your Sarah health and strength and spirits that brighten all the objects around her. Mary Pat is quite recovered from the measles which have been of the most favourable kind, and young Sarah is anxious that her turn should come soon; from little appearances I do not think she will have long to wait...'

Clearly Collingwood was enjoying life with his family and he refused the Admiralty when they offered him a ship. He turned them down saying 'I am not desirous of being employed in the sort of service that peace offers.' In other words he was exchanging inactivity at sea for relaxation at home. Collingwood felt he had earned his retirement and the letters he wrote indicate that he would happily have spent the rest of his days on dry land.

Cuthbert had effectively retired and his time was occupied in seeing to the 'improvement' of his home in Morpeth. He told his friend Dr Carlyle:

'I have workmen opening out the back part of the premises.. pulling down walls.. creating a field.. to improve our prospect from the house down to the River Wansbeck.'

On his health he commented:

'I do not hear as well as I did formerly, I do not see as well as I did formerly and can scarce read without spectacles. In ten years I think I shall be as old a man as you are now [Dr Carlyle was 80 at the time] but this is a subject I contemplate with pleasure rather than regret. To live a good life has been my care, ever since I had a care: to live a long one has never given me a thought.'

In January 1803 a collier delivered Collingwood's belongings from Spithead to the River Tyne, and when he collected them, he discovered a stray dog in the hold. The mongrel was immediately adopted by the Admiral and christened Bounce. This was just the companion he needed for strolling along the banks of the Wansbeck or for striding through his estates in the Cheviot Hills.

Sadly, for Cuthbert Collingwood and the nation, the Treaty of Amiens lasted one week short of a year. Napoleon Bonaparte had agreed to the peace but he had an ulterior motive. The French dictator wanted a breathing space in which to prepare for an invasion of Britain. Collingwood was aware that neither he, nor the

Collingwood's beloved Cheviots

country, would be settling for a peaceful life after all. At this time he wrote to his friend Dr Carlyle and expressed his fears when he told him 'we are again threatened with war, and all its miseries. I have little hope that it can be avoided.'

On the 3rd of June 1803, two months after his letter to the doctor, he was back on board ship. The Friday morning saw him hoisting his flag in *HMS Diamond*, a frigate. His first task was to join Admiral Cornwallis at Brest on the French coast. As he departed England, with Bounce at his side, Collingwood was no doubt anxious to finish the job to end the war and return home. As he got on with the nation's business, did it occur to him that he would never return to Morpeth and his beloved garden? Or that he had seen his wife and family for the last time? When he reached his destination, Cornwallis was delighted and greeted his arrival with the words 'Here comes my old friend Collingwood, the last to leave my fleet and the first to join me.' It was fortunate that the two like-minded officers were firm friends and this meeting would have softened Collingwood's disappointment at leaving his loved ones.

At the blockade post, Collingwood was allocated the *Venerable* but almost as soon as he was settled into the ship, he was moved to another. This would become a pattern as the Admiralty sent Collingwood from ship to ship to check out their efficiency. He told his father-in-law: 'The Admiral sends all ships to me' and whilst that was a tribute to Collingwood's skills at assessing their sea-worthiness and fighting potential, it was an unsatisfactory arrangement for Collingwood the commander. The 'changes in subordinates' became extremely wearing. From experience he knew that it took a sustained period of time for a ship to yield its capabilities. The vessel and its crew, needed to be tested under all conditions and it might take weeks and months to create the vital teamwork. Collingwood believed this could only be achieved through drills, routine and consistent leadership.

The blockaded French harbour at Brest, with its two entrances far apart, meant that it was necessary to keep a double watch for enemy arrivals. Collingwood was kept extremely busy and he barely had a moment to himself. When he could snatch a few minutes away from his responsibilities he reached for his pen and wrote home:

> 'Brest is a station of great anxiety and requires constant care and look out, so that I have often been a week without taking my clothes off, and sometimes I am up on the deck a whole night.'

After the demands of the early weeks of his posting, he was more than happy to hand over the supervision of the squadron to another officer. He had been overworked but now he could look to the needs of the *Venerable* where he returned on the 9th August. If Collingwood felt there would be respite aboard his ship, then he was sadly mistaken, for the patrolling of the *Venerable* along the coast called for the utmost attention as 'the tides and the rocks have more danger in them than a battle once a week.' He must have wondered if the fates were against him for his next order was to bring in the ship for replenishing. Collingwood was just getting used to the particular quirks of the vessel and the men were getting used to his authority when there was disruption once more:

> 'I came in from sea with orders from the Admiral to refresh my ship's company, and, poor creatures, they have been almost worked to death ever since. We began by discovering slight defects and the further we went in the examination the more important they appeared until at last she was discovered to be so rotten as to be unfit for sea. We had been sailing for the last six months with only a sheet of copper between us and eternity. I have written to Lord St Vincent to ask him for a sounder ship but it deranges me exceedingly to be thus for ever changing.'

With a heavy heart he was on the move yet again, this time to the *Minotaur*, where he would wait for the return of his vessel, 'for I do not expect to go into port until the conclusion of war.'

Napoleon had resumed the preparations for invasion on a grand scale and at Boulogne the Emperor began amassing his biggest ever army estimated to number around 115,000. Collingwood and the nation were naturally disconcerted by the military activity in France and this was compounded when it was believed Spain was being drawn into the enemy camp. It was reported that Spanish ships were sending supplies into the French ports to assist Bonaparte's navy and Collingwood was adamant that the Royal Navy would 'not allow this friendly aid to be given.' The Rear-Admiral questioned the loyalty and neutrality of the 'Dons':

> 'Where do they stand? We requested a little sand off the beaches to scour our decks but they would not permit it, is this being friendly to us?'

Collingwood did not doubt that a combined force of Spain and France would be difficult to resist, and that the military would be formidable, but he still had supreme confidence in the Royal Navy's ability to repel invaders. However, he did feel increasing disquiet that the enemy seemed to be growing in strength whilst the British authorities appeared to be complacent. Collingwood was right to be concerned at the state of the fleet; the terrible condition of *Venerable* seemed to point directly to a government that had overlooked the needs of its warships in an attempt to make economies. The political leaders had anticipated a period of peace and had allowed the ships to become neglected. The country was free of the rigours of war and Collingwood maintained that this was precisely the time for strengthening:

'We have seldom been able to muster more than fourteen or fifteen ships here at Brest while the French have twenty complete in all things. Now if they were to come out, even if we got the advantage of them with this fleet, it is not likely to be such a victory as is necessary to the country at this time. Nothing short of exterminating them whenever they appear should be the ideal, and we should have a force equal to it. They should be repulsed with such exemplary vengeance as may deter them from any future attempt to subjugate our country. We should give an example to all nations on how to preserve their independence.'

Collingwood's opinions were in complete harmony with Nelson who echoed his friend's sentiments at a later date:

'It is annihilation that the country wants and not merely a splendid victory that would be honourable to the parties concerned. We must bring Bonaparte to his marrow-bones: only numbers can annihilate.'

Napoleon Bonaparte, at the time of Nelson's reflections, was teaching his enemies the meaning of total war by steadily building up France's fighting capacity.

Collingwood spent Christmas ashore at Plymouth whilst he waited for his latest ship to be fitted out for him. His next change of ship was the famous battle-hardened *Culloden* that had seen distinguished service for over twenty years, mainly with the celebrated Captain Troubridge at the helm. Collingwood had not long been on board *Culloden* when he heard of the death of Sir Edward Blackett, one of his favourite correspondents. His death was followed by that of Mrs Carlyle, the doctor's wife and close friend of Sarah. Collingwood's status on his ships inevitably kept him apart from his men; some of his peers described him as cold and aloof. The rear Admiral certainly felt that he needed to keep a distance from his crew and that overfamiliarity was bad for discipline. At times it must have been an effort for Collingwood to contain his thoughts and feelings but at least he had the release mechanism of writing to trusted confidants. There was a small group of friends and relations that Cuthbert confided in, and discussed the news and issues of the day, so he must have felt the loss of Blackett very deeply. Clearly Collingwood could not be present at either of his friends' funerals and that must have compounded his grief.

At this sad time he did lean heavily on one of his lieutenants for support, which was out of character for the Northumbrian. John Clavell was the officer that he came to rely on. Clavell, like Nelson, was the son of a parson and at the time he was only twenty-five years of age but he had managed to 'lift the spirits' of Collingwood:

'I was miserable when I first came into this ship, but things are now much mended, and in an orderly state. It has been a laborious job for poor Clavell, but he has done it well.'

There were stories that during an irksome nightwatch at Brest, his lieutenant was by his side and it was said that Clavell had suggested his commander should take to his bed. Collingwood replied 'I must not leave the deck.' The lieutenant tried to convince him there was a good look-out and that he was almost exhausted. Collingwood answered 'I fear *you* are. You have need of rest, so go to bed and I will watch by myself.' Clavell stayed and they dozed fitfully alongside each other beside a cannon and stirred only to sweep the horizon with their night-glasses, anxious that the enemy should not escape in the dark.

The next six months passed by with interminable tedium as the British fleet watched the French coast and peered into the ports for any sign of action. As the watching and waiting continued, Collingwood reflected on the European situation as he saw it, and his comments in his letters home were as perceptive as ever:

A STOPPAGE to a STRIDE over the GLOBE

Napoleon astride the world

'Of peace with France, I see no prospect, nothing less than another revolution in that country can rescue Europe from the tyranny of a military despot; but God knows whether even that would be more than changing one tyrant for another. The army of France is everything - the people nothing, but they are necessary to the support of that army, which is a complete subversion of order, and the most melancholy state to which society can be reduced.'

He was not optimistic for the future, as he believed:

'This dilatory war they carry on with us looks as though it will continue for a term of years; and there is no power in Europe now of consequence enough to say that the peace of mankind shall no longer be disturbed. Russia cannot; Prussia will not; Austria dare not. All the rest must do as they are ordered.'

In the crucial first five years of the 19th century it seemed that England stood alone.

In the long weary months of duty, Collingwood shared his thoughts with father-in-law, John Erasmus Blackett:

'Admiral Cornwallis has left us and I dare say he is heartily tired of this cruising, as everybody must be of such a life. It is only the safety of our country that makes us support such a deprivation of everything which is pleasurable but whenever we are blessed with peace, I shall go ashore with extreme satisfaction, never to embark again.'

His thoughts were constantly of home for he added:

'My chief anxiety is to see my daughters well and virtuously educated. I am much obliged to them for weeding my oaks. I have a nurseryman here from Ryton [Northumberland] who was pressed into service. It is a great pity that they should press such a man just because he went to sea for a short time when he was younger. They have broken up his business at home, distressed his family, and sent him here, where he is of little or no service. I grieve for him, poor man!'

The ruthless press gangs

He continued, and commented on a subject that was something of a hobby horse, the shortage of timber for ship building:

'You might be surprised to hear that most of the joints which were used in the *Hibernia* were taken from Spanish ships that were captured on 14th February [1797] and what they could not furnish was supplied by iron. I wish everyone thought on this subject as I do; if they did, they would walk through their farms with their pockets full of acorns and drop them in the hedge sides and let them take their chance.'

His 'heart of oak' campaign became something of a personal crusade, for Collingwood had never known a time when the Royal Navy had not experienced a tree shortage. The island nation could not meet the demand and Collingwood was famous for planting acorns at every opportunity. It is said that the large amount of oaks in the town of Morpeth is due to their famous sea-faring resident. His oak plantation in College Valley, which is still in evidence, grew very slowly and became stunted, but of course Collingwood was investing for the future and he could not have known that the warships - the great 'wooden walls of England' - would be replaced by iron-clad vessels before his oaks would reach maturity.

In January 1805, Admiral Villeneuve and a French fleet squadron of eleven ship-of-the-line and nine frigates came out of Toulon unexpectedly, and Nelson, who was caught off guard, lost sight of them. Two British frigates shadowed the enemy but they were obliged to wait at Sardinia for the rendezvous with Lord Nelson, who took some time to arrive with his squadron. The pursuers were at a loss to discover where the enemy had gone and Horatio sailed up the Italian coastline without success before trying the Greek Islands. That too, was the wrong guess, but whilst he was there he heard that the French Ambassador had been recalled from Constantinople. The move suggested to Nelson that Villeneuve would be taking his ships to Egypt, so he sailed for Alexandria.

Wrong again; it proved to be third time unlucky. The communication network was based largely on often-unreliable word of mouth information (passing ships) or inspired guesswork. In the vast swirling oceans, it was very difficult to connect with a fleet that was doing everything in its power to avoid its pursuers.

In fact, the enemy Commander-in-Chief had been heading for the Caribbean with the intention of disrupting British interests but the Frenchman and his fleet were so inexperienced, and loaded as the ships were with marines, they could not cope with the heavy weather - they had not been able to practice for years! The fleet began to scatter and Villeneuve realised that if Nelson caught them up, the British Admiral would have no difficulty in systematically picking them off and destroying them. The Frenchman felt it was madness to proceed, so after four days he turned around and came back to the security of Toulon, to the chagrin of Horatio.

Nelson was criticised in some quarters for losing sight of the French fleet and becoming involved in a wild goose chase but he defended his actions claiming 'It was never my intention to blockade Toulon, I *wanted* the ships to come out into the open water so that I could have the chance to combat them.' He called Villeneuve 'cowardly' because he would not meet him face to face but the enemy commander was very sensible for he knew better then to take on a naval icon who was greatly feared by his opponents.

Cuthbert understood his friend's tactics of standing off. Collingwood's role was slightly different at Brest because under these circumstances it was necessary for the enemy to see the British as a constant physical presence. The menace of the cruising warships was a deadly deterrent. Nelson's intention was to keep his main fleet out of sight of the enemy - as far as fifty miles from the shore, beyond the horizon. They could be signalled at a minute's notice, via a staggered flag system, and they could move in for the attack. Clearly Nelson was inviting the enemy to break out but it was a risky tactic - as demonstrated by Nelson's fruitless pursuit. Of course, if the ploy had worked, it would have been yet another heroic triumph for East Anglia's most famous son.

Martinique 2004

On the 30th March 1805 Villeneuve escaped with his ships from Toulon and once again he outwitted Nelson's watch. On this occasion he was under orders from the highest authority to carry out what

73

Napoleon called his 'Grand Design'. The Emperor had instructed his naval force in the West Indies to meet at Martinique in early July and their information was that Admiral Villeneuve would arrive to join them. Admiral Ganteaume had a force at Ferrol, the chief naval station in Spain, and he too was ordered to bring out his ships to the same destination, where, if the plan was successful, there would be a massive gathering of forty-five ships-of-the-line. These formidable fighting vessels would then return en masse to the British waters, sweeping aside everything in its wake. The weight of numbers would guarantee an uninterrupted passage to Boulogne, where they would collect the waiting troops. The military would join the thousands of marines already on board and would, according to Napoleon, prove to be an irresistible force for the invasion of England. That was the Grand Design.

The plan was simple and in principle, a good one. But, Napoleon was a soldier, and whilst his ideas worked well on solid ground, planning a sea campaign was subject to many variables. If the combination of the Spanish and French navies succeeded then the Emperor would have been the unopposed ruler of the Western World, and most of the East. If he failed, then Napoleon could blame the navy. His plan was blind to the vagaries of wind and weather and did not allow for counter moves by the British. He ignored the possibility of confrontation with the enemy until the final showdown, when he assumed the overwhelming power of his combined ships would 'strike a mortal blow'.

Villeneuve, free of Toulon, headed for Cadiz near Gibraltar and made contact with the Spanish Admiral, Gravina, but not all of his fifteen ship-of-the-line were provisioned. He had to leave some behind but most of his heavy warships joined the French fleet on their journey to Martinique in the wide, open seas. Napoleon was delighted when he heard that his ships had escaped so easily from under the nose of Nelson. The first part of the plan was working. Horatio, by now, had information that the enemy were heading for the West Indies with the intention of amassing a huge force, so he went after them. The French admiral eventually arrived at his destination and gathered around him thirty ship-of-the-line. Contrary to Bonaparte's orders, the French squadron based in the Caribbean did

Admiral Gravina

not make the rendezvous and a furious Napoleon 'choked with indignation' when he heard the news. Nevertheless it was still a powerful armada that set off on the return journey back across the Atlantic.

Nelson, who was once again in pursuit, received information that the enemy had sailed into Barbados - wrong again. On arrival he was told that the combined enemy forces were mustering in Martinique. When he learnt of this true destination, he set off immediately; Horatio was desperate for an encounter at sea. By the time he reached Martinique the enemy had left and were heading for home. This suited the enemy, as they knew Nelson would be on their tail and it served their interests to have him floundering about in foreign waters. Villeneuve had a month's start but Horatio was so anxious to catch up with his foe, that he made remarkable time on the journey back, arriving off Gibraltar in July. Villeneuve also got back at the same time but brought his fleet to Ferrol, before sailing south along the coast to join Admiral Gravina's remaining ships at Cadiz.

They were back where they started. Nelson was bitterly disappointed that there had been no battle and he could draw little satisfaction from the chase. The enemy had rounded up a formidable fleet and had been out on the ocean practising drills and seamanship. On arrival, Nelson was relieved to learn that Collingwood had kept everything under control in his absence. He wrote to his friend saying 'I am as you may suppose, miserable at not having fallen in with the enemy fleet' and he added that when his ships were watered and provisioned he 'may pay his old messmate' a visit:

'Not my dear friend to take command from you (for I may probably add mine to you) but to consult how we can best serve our country by detaching a part of this large force.'

Before the meeting could take place, Horatio was asked to return to England and he feared the worst. He felt sure that his inept pursuit would bring criticism from the public and the higher authorities but he could not have been more mistaken. Nelson had not fully appreciated the extent of his own heroic status. 'Nelsonmania' had hit Great Britain and factories were turning out mementoes and souvenirs of his achievements. Plates, pictures, busts, jugs and mugs, anything and everything that could display his image was produced. He might have considered the flight to West Indian waters a failure but the people did not; they admired his determination to go after the enemy against all odds. They celebrated his pursuit. Did he not take his tired and weather-beaten fleet half-way across the world and back at great speed? And didn't the enemy run for their lives? According to newspaper reports, Villeneuve had avoided facing the might of the Royal Navy and his ships were now cowering in a Spanish port. For the moment the nation felt the invasion threat was over, thanks to Horatio, their hero. That is how it was perceived in England.

Collingwood's watching brief had been diligent and dull. Cuthbert would have loved to have been involved in the chase and nothing would have given him greater satisfaction than to have confronted the enemy. Unfortunately, the time had passed slowly for the Rear-Admiral and after fifteen months away from his family he was clearly homesick and unaware of the foreboding events that were a few short months away. As late as the summer 1805, he was writing to Blackett and looking to the following year in which he anticipated the end of his naval career:

'I am fully determined, if I can get home and manage it properly, to go on shore next spring for the rest of my life: for I am very weary. There is no end to my business: I am at work from morning till even; but I dare say Lord Nelson will be out next month. He told me he should: and then what will become of me I don't know. I should wish to go home, but I must go or stay as the exigencies of the times require. This, with all its labour, is a most unprofitable station; but that is not a consideration of much moment to me. What I look to as the first and great object, is to defeat the combined fleet, of whom I can get little information; but I watch them narrowly, and if they come out I will fight them merrily; for on their discomfiture depends the safety of England, and it shall not fail in my hands if I can help it.'

Collingwood admired the French ship builders and readily admitted: 'line for line, their vessels are better than ours' but he added that 'the enemy was weaker, not in ships or in courage, but in leadership.' Collingwood was aware that two thirds of their trained and experienced officers had been butchered during the 'Reign of Terror' and the enemy fleet would not regain their confidence if they remained bottled up in a harbour. Cuthbert wrote:

'Each time they break out and engage our squadrons, they learn a little more and grow steadily more confident - even if a victory is denied them. But, blockading is no longer the answer, in my opinion. It hurts the innocent as much as those for whom it is intended. Clear and decisive action is the solution. Hit the enemy whenever and wherever you can, the size of action is immaterial.'

The British fleet were not happy under Collingwood and he knew it. The frustration he was feeling affected the other ships too; they were all in need of action. They regarded Collingwood as a stern and silent disciplinarian, and at this particularly critical time, he showed none of the kindliness or the quiet humour which his friends and family warmed to in his private life. At his dinner table, conversation was stilted and frivolity discouraged. Navy etiquette demanded that guests would only speak when they were spoken to by their chief. The much-respected Captain William Hoste commented that:

'Old Collingwood likes quiet people; he seems to prefer the company of his beloved dog, Bounce.'

The commander's fleet were, like himself, restless with the mind-numbing watch. Hoste correctly assessed that 'Under the 'old bear' most of his officers were bored beyond measure.' Collingwood kept a close scrutiny on all the potential enemy outlets and he would not allow socialising amongst the ships at this time. He even discouraged his vessels from leaving their post to receive fresh supplies from passing ships. The admiral was a hard taskmaster during this critical period.

On 21 August 1805, whilst Nelson was in England, Collingwood wrote to his wife and told her about a close encounter:

'We were cruising off Cadiz, when down came the entire combined enemy fleet of men-of-war: we were only three poor things, with a frigate and a bomb, and drew off towards the Straits, not very ambitious, as you may suppose, to try our strength against such odds. They followed us with sixteen large ships, so

Cadiz 1910

we retired, but on our approaching the Straits they left us and joined their friends in Cadiz, where they are fitting and replenishing their provisions. We, in our turn, followed them back, and today have been looking into Cadiz, where their fleet is now as thick as a wood. I reckon there are now thirty-six sail-of-the-line and plenty of frigates. What can I do with such a host? But I hope I shall get reinforcement suited to the occasion, and if I do, well betide us!'

He was powerless to act and could only watch from a safe distance although he made sure the information was passed to the Admiralty. Collingwood knew that once fresh ships reached him, Villeneuve's armada, that had settled in the port 'like a forest', could not drive through the straits unchallenged. The Northumbrian believed that, all things being equal, they would never get through at all.

With the knowledge of the build up at Cadiz, Nelson met with King George and the Cabinet and had long discussions with the new Prime Minister. Collingwood was happy to see the re-emergence of William Pitt (the younger) and he wrote that under his political leadership there was the 'promise of a bright future'. Pitt was sympathetic to the needs of the Royal Navy and as Collingwood pointed out:

'These times require talent, which fall to the lot of few men. Perhaps Pitt is the only man in England who can find resources against all the evils we have to encounter.'

Nelson, in his conversations with the PM, persuaded him that British ships should be sent very quickly to attack the enemy. Pitt agreed to Nelson's request then asked:

'Now, who is to take command?'
Nelson replied:
'You cannot have a better man than the present one - Collingwood.'
The suggestion was brushed aside by the Prime

William Pitt the Younger

Minister who told Nelson emphatically,
 'No, that won't do. You must take command.'
Horatio's objections were overruled. Pitt then asked:
 'Can you be ready in three days?'
Lord Nelson answered,
 'I am ready now.'

Nelson sent a message to his friend ahead of his arrival:
 'My Dear Coll, I shall be with you in a few days and I hope you will be my
 second in command.'
There were those who felt Collingwood might have been resentful of the
younger man's rise to leadership but nothing could have been further from the
truth. Cuthbert Collingwood was aware that with Nelson leading from the front,
the chances of success would be greatly improved. He had no illusions about his
own ability and if he had been asked to take on the role of Commander-in-Chief
he would willingly have done his duty. There was no jealousy directed towards
his friend, in fact it was the reverse, he was overjoyed, for together they would
make a formidable partnership. They both had the same aims and outlook and
they would share the plan of attack. Nelson told Collingwood:
 'We are one and I hope we always shall be.'
In Nelson's letter he also informed Cuthbert that he would be transferring to
another ship - again! 'You will change from the *Dreadnought* to the *Royal
Sovereign* which I hope you will like.' Collingwood's heart probably sank at the
thought of changing ships yet again but Nelson was actually doing his friend a
good turn. At the time, the *Royal Sovereign* was a notoriously slow sailer and was
known in the fleet as the 'West Country Wagon' but on delivery Collingwood
was delighted to see that the old ship was newly-coppered. The plating around
the hull had streamlined the *Royal Sovereign*; it was transformed and ideal for
Rear-Admiral Collingwood, the sailing master.
 Nelson arrived very quietly to join the fleet, without the usual fanfare. There
was no 'piping' on board or gunnery salutes; he did not want the opposition to
be alerted. The name of Nelson had the power to strike fear into the enemy and
he did not wish to deter them from coming out. He immediately discussed the
situation with Collingwood; Nelson knew that Cuthbert's judgement and opinion
would be invaluable. Nelson valued the intimacy of their long-standing friendship
but he also embraced a collective outlook. Horatio had described his captains as
a 'band of brothers' at the Battle of the Nile and his style of leadership was based
on camaraderie and motivation. It was said that Cuthbert Collingwood was too
rigid and unwavering but he believed a firm authority was required during the
blockading period. He never spared himself and he expected the same high
commitment from his subordinates, and although there may have been discontent
amongst the ranks, even the most grudging could not deny that nothing slipped
past the Rear-Admiral. He did not expect popularity but he did expect his
charges to place iron duty before personal pleasure. When Nelson arrived the

officers were desperate for some light relief - and he supplied it.

Lord Nelson's timing was perfect. He realised the spirits of the fleet needed lifting and he was welcomed with open arms. His mere presence was a tonic and a reassurance and he immediately encouraged visits between ships - a move Collingwood had resisted. On board his flag ship *Victory* he invited his captains over to dine so that he could openly explain his ideas on how he proposed to fight the expected battle. This was an innovative approach; usually the commander sent a written memorandum to his captains which described the detailed tactics. By taking the men into his confidence, Horatio made them feel valued and an essential member of a team. His warm reception delighted Nelson as he told Emma:

The 'Nelson Touch'

'I believe my arrival was most welcome not only to Commander Collingwood but also to every individual in the fleet, and when I came to explain the 'Nelson Touch' [the tactics] it was like an electric shock. Some shed tears, all approved - it was new - it was singular - it was simple!' and from Admirals downwards it was repeated - 'it must succeed, if ever they will allow us to get at them! You are my lord, surrounded by friends whom you inspire with confidence.'

The battle plan, which Horatio discussed with his captains, was no secret; he had openly demonstrated his intentions on Lord Sidmouth's dining room table in England. In essence, his plan was to avoid the indecisive, old-fashioned and unsatisfactory style of conflict. His aim was total defeat of the enemy and this would be achieved by the innovative plan to use three columns, one under his own direction and another under his second in command. A third division was to be held in reserve to be employed as he decided:

'I shall go at them at once, if I can, about one third of their line from the leading ship. What do you think of it? I'll tell you what I think of it. I think it will surprise and confound the enemy! They won't know what I am about. It will bring forward a pell-mell battle and that is what I want.'

At the heart of the plan was Nelson's instruction that his captains use their initiative. Initiative was a word that was rarely uttered in the Royal Navy but Nelson was actually encouraging it. The strict adherence to orders was a feature of all battle campaigns and this also applied to the French and Spanish fleets. To offer his captains this freedom of action within the conflict had an inspirational effect amongst the leaders in the fleet and to a man they were determined to show Nelson that his confidence in their abilities was not misplaced. He had spent hours discussing the detail of the attack with Collingwood. They had both experienced a pell-mell action at St Vincent and they drew up the plan from their shared personal knowledge.

His French opponent, Admiral Villeneuve, knew of Nelson's intentions and had discussed counter proposals with his staff. He wrote before Trafalgar:

HMS Victory

> 'The enemy will try to double our rear, cut through the line, and bring against the ships thus isolated, groups of his own. Captains must rely on their courage and love of glory, rather than the signals of the admiral, who may be already engaged and wrapped up in smoke. The captain who is not in action is not at his post.'

The Frenchman and his Spanish allies anticipated the pell-mell battle that Nelson had wished for and at Trafalgar he had a very ingenious defence system that almost worked, to counteract the Royal Navy assault.

Nelson's personality and self-assurance was infectious. The simple gesture of encouraging his officers was enough to win their hearts and minds after the recent tedium. Horatio's attitude differed from that of Collingwood, so it was fortunate that they were devoted friends of very long standing. Nelson admitted:

> 'No subordinate could possibly have been more welcoming, so without jealousy, or such a rock of solidarity. Coll is as perfect as could be expected.'

Cuthbert Collingwood may have been out of favour with the fleet but Nelson knew his worth. They continued their affectionate intimacy and Nelson noted in his log [9 October] that he had sent his second-in-command what they both referred to, as the 'Nelson Trunk', a box to which each had a key. By means of this they could exchange memoranda, notes and papers.

It was common knowledge that Collingwood did not care for his own flag captain, Edward Rotherham, but he appeared to be stuck with him. Rotherham was born in Hexham in 1752 and was a fellow Northumbrian. He was the son of a doctor and had started his early career working on the River Tyne colliers. Rotherham had been a lieutenant at the 'Glorious First of June' but it was beyond Collingwood's comprehension as to how he had risen to flag captain status. A contemporary described him as 'fat and stupid' and there is a description in a memoir of Hercules Robinson who was a midshipman on Collingwood's ships:

> 'On one occasion when the captain had committed some monstrous blunder, and after the usual bowing and formality, which Lord Collingwood never omitted, the chief said 'Captain, I have been thinking, whilst I looked at you, how strange it is that a man should grow so big and know so little. That's all, sir, that's all.' And with further bows and courteous formality the chief turned and left.'

Collingwood clearly did not suffer fools and would probably be described today as a control freak; it must have been difficult for subordinates to meet his very high standards. It was said that his flag captains were lonely creatures and much criticised. Nelson must have been aware of his second-in-command's frosty relationship with his captain for he did what he could to lighten the situation by inviting them both to dinner. It evidently did not soften Cuthbert but Horatio attempted to give Rotherham a confidence-boost which his admiral seemed to be undermining.

Another change that Nelson brought about was the method of watching the port. As ordered, Collingwood had kept the visible blockade to bottle up the enemy, but now Nelson withdrew. He kept his main fleet out of sight from the shore and hoped to lure the enemy into the open sea. On the 9th October he sent a copy of his battle plan to Collingwood with a note:

'I wish to place you perfectly at ease respecting my intentions, and to give full scope to your judgement to carry them into effect. We can, my dear Coll, have no little jealousies. We have only one great object in view, that of annihilating our enemies, and getting a glorious peace for our country. No man has more confidence in another than I have with you: and no man will render your services more justice than your very old friend, Nelson and Bronte.'

Over the next ten days Collingwood met with Nelson and they weighed up the situation. On the 19th October Horatio extended the invitation once more and sent the message:

'What a beautiful day! Will you be tempted out of your ship?'

Collingwood was unable to accept the invitation. He would later write:

'Before a reply could be sent to the *Victory* the signal was made that the French were coming out of Cadiz, and we chased immediately'.

The battle began in two days and the pair did not meet again in this lifetime.

The Battle of Trafalgar commences

VICE-ADMIRAL COLLINGWOOD
Action and Aftermath

We'll fight and we'll conquer again and again.

It was thirty-three Royal Navy vessels against the thirty-six of the combined enemy. Collingwood felt the odds were not too difficult but had he known the dissention that existed in Cadiz amongst the French and Spanish admirals not to mention the officers and men, the Northumbrian would have taken heart and believed, quite rightly, that the odds favoured Britain.

In the *Royal Sovereign*, Rear-Admiral Collingwood began the day as calmly as any other. Whilst he was shaving he asked a servant if he had noticed any ships yet. The man pushed his head out of the dimly lit cabin and reported that he could just see a crowd of ships through the mist. He answered 'Then we'll soon see a good deal more of them' and continued shaving. Collingwood dressed with particular care that morning and when he saw Lieutenant Clavell he told him:

'You had better put silk stockings on as I have done, for if you should get a shot in the leg, it would be so much more manageable for the surgeon.'

It was typical of Cuthbert's clinical attention to detail and forward thinking that he should be considering the possibility of amputation. Collingwood had been described by several of his peers as a 'cold fish' but he needed a clear head, and in this life or death situation, he would not allow fear or emotion to cloud his judgement. Captain Rotherham appeared on deck in full dress uniform, complete with a large cocked hat. He had always fought in his most showy attire and today would be no exception. The captain may not have been Collingwood's favourite but no one doubted his tenacity in battle - he was up for it and would fight like a tiger. The captain, like his admiral, had been born a Northumbrian and the crew of the *Royal Sovereign* contained many proud Newcastle volunteers. Collingwood emanated authority and confidence and there were many local seamen who had chosen to go into battle alongside the celebrated Tyneside leader. The Rear-Admiral was delighted to report that:

'The men from the River Tyne are a set of stout young men and a great addition to my strength, my ship being now so well-manned that I cannot say I have any anxiety to change her.'

Collingwood's last task before occupying the forward poop deck was to visit the gun levels and talk with his men. He gathered his officers together and addressed them briefly on the task that lay ahead. Collingwood was not a man to waste words and his final message was short, but inspirational. He told them:

'Now, gentlemen, let us do something today which the world may talk of hereafter.'

Collingwood, with his copper-bottomed warship, took advantage of his own vessel's superior sailing to lead the attack on the enemy rearguard. He led his division by a number of ship lengths, as he cut through the water, anxious to combat the opposition as soon as possible. As he drove forward, the latest of many signals came from Nelson's flagship. The closeness of the enemy and tension of the situation caused Collingwood to reply with irritation:

'What on earth is Nelson signalling about? We all know what we have to do.'

On board the *Victory* it is reported that Nelson at about a quarter to noon, had said to his captain: 'I shall now amuse myself with a signal' and he called over his signalman telling him:

'Mr Pasco, I want you to convey to the fleet 'England confides that every man will do his duty.' You must be quick for I have one more signal to add.'

Pasco replied:

'If your Lordship will permit me to substitute 'expects' for 'confides' the signal will sooner be completed because the word 'expects' is in the signal book, and 'confides' must be spelt with many more flags.

Nelson answered:

'That will do Pasco, make it directly.'

The most famous signal in naval history had to be translated by officers and communicated to the lower deck. It was said that when Collingwood finally heard the message he was delighted and found the words inspirational. He insisted that his officers pass on their commander's words of encouragement and the account claims that 'the men's cheers resounded around the gun decks.' The

England Expects That Every Man Will Do His Duty.

reality of the situation would have been quite different since the crew of the *Royal Sovereign* and the fleet itself, contained Americans, Germans, Dutch, Swiss and even Spaniards and Frenchmen amongst the largely British crew. Most would be stripped to the waist, with handkerchiefs around their heads to stop the sweat getting into their eyes and their ears would be plugged with rags to deaden the noise of the guns. It is unlikely that the message ever reached them. On *Victory* the thirty-two bits of bunting needed for the message were then replaced by a white flag with a blue cross and a red, white and blue tri-colour. These two flags were known as Number 16 and were instantly recognisable as 'Close Action' - in other words: 'Let battle commence!'

Close action!

The enemy guns began at 10:45am and they were directed towards the *Royal Sovereign*. The range of the heaviest 32-pound cannon was one-and-a-half miles and the weight [14.4kg] referred to the 32-pound ball or 'shot' that was being unleashed. Seven or eight enemy ships fired at Collingwood's leading vessel but they were well out of range and knew they were unlikely to strike the ship. However their opening salvos were not wasted as they were using their initial shots to calibrate the distances so that when the *Royal Sovereign* came closer they would be more certain of hitting their mark. An hour later the firing began in earnest as Collingwood drove towards the *Santa Anna*. The plan was to cut through the waiting enemy line and turn to attack a specified ship. The *Santa Anna* was the second largest ship afloat at 122-guns and that was Collingwood's target in his three-decker with two dozen fewer muzzles.

By now the British vessels had cleared the gun decks for action and their hammocks and belongings were stowed in netting around the perimeter of the ship's decks as added protection from the enemy's musket balls. Each cross yardarm on the masts was chained into place to prevent it from falling onto the men below. The French aimed chain shot into their opponents rigging in order to dismast and cripple them. These deadly projectiles were cannonballs joined by a chain so that they spread out when fired and scythed into sails and sailors. A ship without sail or means of escaping was more likely to surrender. The British approach, which their enemy felt was dishonourable, was to direct their gunnery into the hulls and create sufficient damage and human carnage to

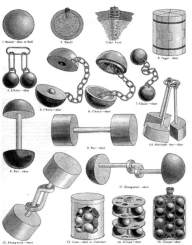

Deadly cannon fodder

encourage submission. This method required very close contact and naturally the men were terrified, as they lay semi-naked, staring out of open gun ports, waiting for the bedlam to begin. As a seaman wrote at the time:

'The din of battle I can endure, but the waiting is torture.'

All hatches had marines positioned alongside with orders to shoot any men who attempted to leave their post and run for safety.

Behind the *Royal Sovereign* was the *Belleisle*, some way back. An officer of the marines on board Captain Hargood's following vessel vividly described the tension which would have been apparent in both ships:

'As we were steering directly for them we could only be passive, and perseveringly approach the position we were to occupy in this great battle. This was a trying moment. Captain Hargood had taken his station on the forepart of the quarterdeck whence he issued orders for the men to lie down at their quarters, and with the utmost coolness he directed the steering of the ship.

The silence on board was almost awful, broken only by the firm voice of the captain, 'steady!' or 'starboard a little!' which was repeated by the master to the quarter master at the helm, and occasionally by an officer calling to the impatient men: 'Lie down there, you, sir!' As we got nearer and nearer to the enemy the silence was, however, broken frequently by the sadly stirring shrieks of the wounded and the dying. We had more than fifty killed or injured before we fired a shot; and our colours were three times shot away and re-hoisted during that time.

Seeing our men were falling fast, the first lieutenant ventured to ask the captain if he had not better show his broadside to the enemy and fire, if only to cover the ship in smoke. The gallant commander's reply was somewhat stern, but emphatic:

'No. We are ordered to go through the line, and go through we shall, by God!'

For twenty minutes or so the experienced officers kept up the spirits of the men around them by observing, 'We should soon begin our work', when – like as on any other occasion the welcome order was given, 'Up guards, and at 'em!' our energies were joyfully called into play by 'Stand to your guns.'

An account by the young Lieutenant Standish captured the terrible ferocity of the battle:

'Shrieks and cries of agony filled the air as the deadly shot came over from the enemy and the remains of bodies, broken and incomplete, lay about the upper decks.'

The officer was so horrified, that he too, was about to lie flat on the deck, like many of his colleagues - from fear, not by order. He looked across to his brave captain, resisted the temptation, and stayed on his feet. He would later write of his commander:

'The serenity of his countenance and the composure with which he paced the deck, drove more than half my

The gun deck of Victory

terrors away, and, joining him, I became suffused with his spirit, which cheered me on to act the part that became me. My experience is an instance of how much depends upon the example of those in command when exposed to the fire of the enemy, more particularly in the trying situation in which we were placed for nearly thirty minutes, from not having the power to retaliate.'

The description of the courageous Captain Hargood would have applied equally to Collingwood's leadership although the *Royal Sovereign* did fire at the enemy to use her own smoke as a shield.

Under tremendous fire, Collingwood ordered 'all sail' towards the *Santa Anna* and as he did so, the *Fougueux* guessed Collingwood's intentions. The French ship began closing the gap between himself and that of the *Santa Anna*. The English admiral's response was immediate and he ordered Rotherham to steer directly at the extended bowsprit of the French ship, intending to smash it aside. The *Fougueux* capitulated and backed her top main sail to allow the *Royal Sovereign* to pass through. Collingwood took advantage of the retreat and as he passed behind the *Santa Anna* he declared that the enemy's ship was 'a Spanish perfection' and he later wrote 'she towered over the *Royal Sovereign* like a castle.' In spite of his admiration he sent a volley of raking shots through her stern. Admiral Alava, on board the enemy ship, admitted that one broadside had killed 350 of his men. By the time Collingwood had turned the *Royal Sovereign* to face the enemy's port side, *Santa Anna* was unable to cope with the relentless fire. The Rear-Admiral's master gunners were firing three broadsides every four minutes to a single reply every seven or eight minutes.

After a quarter of an hour of unremitting action it looked as though the Spanish vessel had succumbed and Rotherham shook Collingwood by the hand. In a moment of mutual respect he told his fellow Northumbrian: 'I congratulate you, Sir, she is slackening her fire, and must soon strike.' The crew certainly expected the *Santa Anna* to lower her flag and there was the real possibility of the *Royal Sovereign* receiving the sword of Admiral Alava in surrender, before any other British ship had engaged the enemy. The Spanish admiral clung on hoping that he would receive assistance, which he did, as the *Fougueux* placed herself at the rear of the *Royal Sovereign* and two other ships fired at her bow. The onslaught from the enemy ships did not deter Collingwood as he was defiantly seen striding around the high deck. A contemporary description of the scene was recalled by Hercules Robinson, midshipman:

'Dear old Cuddie (as we called him) was walking the break in the poop with his little triangular, gold-laced, cocked hat and wearing his silk stockings and buckled shoes. He was musing over the progress of the fight and munching on an apple. At length he went down to the quarterdeck and joined the men, encouraging them not to 'fire a shot in waste'. Admiral Collingwood looked himself along the guns to see that they were properly pointed, and commending the sailors, particularly a black man, who was afterwards killed, but who, while the admiral stood beside him, fired ten times directly into the porthole of the *Santa Anna*. It was like being in the heart of a volcano - with five ships around us - yet Collingwood had a single-handed coolness that he showed all day. A large part of the crew on board were men from the Tyne and they stood by their man.'

Collingwood took no satisfaction in the carnage; he just wanted the enemy to accept defeat so that the punishment could cease. In the course of the close-action he engaged with five of the enemy ships and since the *Royal Sovereign* was shrouded in her own smoke, the opposition were firing into each other in an early demonstration of the destructive effect of 'friendly fire'.

Before transferring to the *Royal Sovereign*, Collingwood had trained his previous crew on board *Dreadnought* to release three broadsides every three-and-a-half minutes, and this rapidity of fire would be a major factor in the battle's outcome. The *Dreadnought's* gunnery under a different commander was still a very effective warship. After the first battle exchanges the *Dreadnought* entered the action and adopted a roving, supporting role. Her firepower would break the heart of the enemy with her devastating bombardments.

In the sea battles of the Napoleonic era, it was rare for the wooden ships to be sunk; they could be severely damaged but not beyond repair. There was the famous incident at the Battle of the Nile, when the powder room of *L'Orient* caught alight and the ship exploded into oblivion but that was exceptional. Mostly the ships struck their colours because they had been raked from end to end and their guns had been dismounted; or they had taken too many casualties; or they had been boarded and overrun; or because their masts and rigging had been shot away and they were helpless. Battles at sea were grim beyond belief. Collingwood, who thought he had battered the *Santa Anna* into submission during the first twenty minutes of action, continued firing into her with deadly accuracy for the next two hours before finally she gave up. He admitted 'Not a ship fired into her except ourselves and you have no conception how completely she was ruined.' The *Royal Sovereign* also suffered badly; her masts and yards were destroyed so that she could no longer be controlled. Collingwood was forced to signal to the *Euryalus* to take him in tow. Before receiving assistance the Rear-Admiral had welcomed a lieutenant from the *Santa Anna* on board the *Royal Sovereign* and the sword of surrender was handed over. On arrival the officer asked the name of the ship and was told it was the *Royal Sovereign* in his broken English he said, as he patted one of the guns, 'It should have been named the 'Royal Devil'. The first eight ships in Collingwood's division fought seventeen of the enemy and they captured five, crippled four more and drove two more out of the line. Collingwood from his perspective said:

'It was a battle planned by officers but won by sailors. It is the most decisive and complete victory ever gained against an enemy.'

The second-in-command had wiped out the enemy's rear - half the fleet - and victory was all but assured.

But what of Lord Nelson who was attacking the van? It was inevitable that the leading ships would have to withstand a terrible concentration of fire and Horatio and the ships close behind him took tremendous punishment from the enemy's broadsides. As the *Victory* cut through the line, there was a period when the ship was at the mercy of Villeneuve. The French commander knew that Nelson would never tolerate an action in the formal tradition, of guns verses guns, and he also knew that if a 'pell-mell' battle was allowed to happen, then nothing could save his fleet. He poured heavy fire into the approaching ships, aiming high to strike at masts at rigging in the hope of disabling their rivals. Nelson was leading from the front and at 12:24pm, after coming under fire for fifteen minutes, the commander finally ordered his men to 'Open fire!'

One of first casualties was Nelson's secretary, John Scott. A ship's secretary was a dangerous occupation at the time of battle. They had to be on the quarter deck or poop deck alongside the commander to write down his instructions and to record orders and note their timings. Secretaries were very vulnerable as they were static whilst they were writing and could be an easy target for enemy snipers. The unfortunate clerk was struck by a cannonball that almost cut him in two. His body must have been badly mangled for Nelson was shocked and asked uncertainly: 'Is that poor Scott?' Before Horatio could commiserate the Captain of the Marines rushed forward and ordered the secretary's body to be thrown overboard immediately. It was not good for morale to see mutilated corpses on the decks and it was accepted practice to throw the dead directly into the sea.

As they approached 'close action' the French ship *Neptune* raked the *Victory* and her upper decks were temporarily out of action although the lower deck was firing full broadsides. Nelson's luck would have appeared to have run out, for he came face to face with the 74-gun *Redoubtable* regarded as the best trained ship in the enemy fleet. Captain Jean Lucas had the foresight to see that the British flagship was disabled on the higher gun levels so he shut down his own lower gun ports and concentrated his devastating fire on the upper tiers. *Redoubtable* and *Victory* were locked together as their rigging became entangled and Nelson had no room to manoeuvre since his wheel had been shot away. Both crews were anxious to board for hand-to-hand fighting but the English muskets of the marines kept the French back. The famous old warship the 'fighting *Temeraire*' (depicted in her final days by the artist J M W Turner) came to Nelson's aid and fired into the other side of the *Redoubtable*. Lucas had been getting the upper hand against *Victory* and they had thrown the grapnels ready to board; the signalling trumpet had even been sounded. But the *Temeraire* tipped the balance as the French captain wrote after the event:

'It would be difficult to describe the horrible carnage caused by the murderous broadside. More than 200 of our brave lads were killed or wounded. A little later a third ship stationed herself astern of *Redoubtable* and fired into us at pistol range; in less than half an hour

Captain Lucas of Redoubtable

our ship was so riddled that she seemed to be no more than a mass of wreckage. In this state the *Temeraire* hailed us to strike and not prolong a useless resistance. The entire stern was stove-in, the rudder-stock, the tiller, were shot to pieces. All the guns were shattered by the shots, or from ships having run us aboard. An 18-pounder gun on the main deck and a 36-pound carronade on the forecastle having burst, killed and wounded many of our people. On the two sides of the ship, all the lids and bars of the ports were utterly cut to pieces. Four of our six pumps were shattered, as well as our ladders in general, so that communication between decks and the upper works was extremely difficult. All the decks were covered with dead, buried beneath the debris and the splinters from the different parts of the ship. Out of the ship's company of 643 men, we had 522 disabled, 300 being killed and 222 wounded, with whom the orlop [lowest] deck was thronged; yet still they cried, 'Vive l'Empereur! We're not taken yet. Is our captain still alive?'

It was only when it was reported the leaks in *Redoubtable* had left his ship terminally foundering that, with the greatest reluctance, he decided to strike:

'At the instant I was assured of this, I ordered the colours to be hauled down.'

The Victory and the Redoubtable meet head on

Lucas and his crew had done their job well but it was one of the expertly trained French marines who would have the greatest impact. It was half an hour after the engagement of *Redoubtable* and *Victory* that a sniper high in the enemy's mizzenmast pointed his musket at the English admiral. Just before the battle had begun, Captain Hardy had suggested to his commander that the four stars of chivalry, emblazoned on his coat, might make him too conspicuous. Nelson had replied 'No doubt that is true, but this is not the time to be changing it.' Should Nelson have listened to advice? Was it vanity or pride, or both, that prompted Nelson to display his glittering emblems, when a plain blue coat would have been more prudent? Captain Hardy was a large target measuring six-feet-four-inches, a colossal height in the 1800s and the slightly-built Lord Nelson at five-feet-five-inches, were steadily pacing the quarterdeck (it was unwise to stand still) and they were just about to reach their turning

Nelson in his distinctive battle dress

point, when Hardy saw Nelson fall to his knees. The captain bent to hear Nelson utter the dreaded words:

'They have done for me at last, Hardy. My backbone is shot through.'

The musket ball had entered his left shoulder and had lodged in the spine; the proximity of the entangled ships meant that the enemy marksman had found his target from a mere fifteen yards away. In the 'Nelson Room' at the National Maritime Museum, the coat with the bullet hole, is displayed in a cabinet alongside his blood-stained stockings and the fatal downward angle of the lead shot was clearly fired from point-blank range. Nelson, knowing that death was imminent, insisted that his face be covered with a handkerchief as they carried him below to the orlop deck to join the increasing ranks of the injured; he did not want his men to be dispirited by seeing the sight of their wounded leader.

Nelson was made comfortable below the water level, and was effectively removed from the action as the sound of battle raged around his ship. Dr Beatty, who administered his wounds, gave a detailed description of the final hours. Mr Burke, one of the medical assistants, came to Nelson after a while and encouraged him by claiming that the enemy were 'decisively defeated and that he hoped his Lordship would be the bearer of the joyful tidings to his country.'

Nelson had no illusions about his condition:

'It is nonsense, Mr Burke, to suppose I can live: my sufferings are great, but they will soon be over.'

It was over an hour before Hardy could return to Horatio and he reported that the fleet had taken about twelve or fourteen ships. 'Have any of our ships struck?' Nelson wanted to know. Hardy replied 'No, my Lord, there is no fear of that.' This knowledge pacified Horatio and after a while the captain felt compelled to return to the quarterdeck. The Rear-Admiral then insisted that those who were attending to him should go and look after the other wounded for he maintained 'you can do nothing for me.' Fifty minutes later Hardy reported back to Nelson to say that the victory was complete and he was certain fourteen or fifteen had surrendered. This pleased Nelson but he had high expectations:

'That is well, but I bargained for twenty.'

In the same breath he demanded 'Anchor, Hardy, anchor!'

Hardy could see that his friend and leader was failing and incapable of command.

'I suppose my Lord, Admiral Collingwood will now take upon himself the direction of affairs.'

The dying chief was emphatic:

'Not while I live, I hope, Hardy.'

He tried to raise himself but fell back and ordered once again:

'For if I live, I'll anchor.'

The outburst had exerted him and when he spoke

Thomas Hardy, Nelson's captain

90

again he was much more reflective:
'In a few minutes I shall be no more. Don't throw me overboard, Hardy.'
The captain reassured him, 'Oh no, certainly not.'
Horatio told his friend
'Then you know what to do.'
His words were now urgent:
'Take care of poor Lady Hamilton and Horatia'
Then he added the immortal phrase:
'Kiss me Hardy.'
Hardy kissed his cheek and Lord Nelson, clearly in pain, uttered:
'Now I am satisfied. Thank God, I have done my duty.'

In death, Nelson was unwilling to relinquish the command, even though he was powerless to oversee the action. Collingwood had for the previous two-and-a-half hours seen off the threat of the enemy ships and his division had taken the vessels in the enemy's rear line. A boat was sent to Collingwood through the war-torn waters telling him of Nelson's wounds and as soon as he could free himself from the engagement he headed for the *Victory*. In the heat of the battle, which was as pell-mell as Nelson had hoped, he took over command. Although it was essentially every captain for themselves, Collingwood needed to gather the information that was arising from the conflict and he had to direct the signals. Before the battle took place Nelson's tactical memorandum had read:
'Captains are to look to their particular line as their rallying point, but in case signals cannot be seen, or clearly understood, no captain can do very wrong if he places his ship alongside that of his enemy.'
This is how the battle was fought.
Collingwood had guessed from the demeanour of the officer that was sent to him that Nelson was wounded and that the wound was mortal. As soon he arrived on board the *Victory* Collingwood was told that minutes earlier, at around 4:30pm, Lord Nelson had passed away. Cuthbert remembered the signal Horatio had sent two days earlier:
'What a beautiful day! Will you be tempted out of your ship?'
The Northumbrian had been unable to accept the invitation because of the sudden precipitation of events but Collingwood had anticipated sharing a victory bottle of claret with his old friend. The loss of a comrade so close to him, closer than any other in the service, affected him deeply. Tears were seen on his cheeks, and this was unheard of, for the stoical admiral was renowned for never showing emotions of any kind. Soon afterwards he would write to Mrs Mary Moutray, now a widow and living with her family in Ireland, and reflect on the days when his friendship with the younger Horatio developed. He described his thoughts when he learnt of his friend's injury:
'It was about the middle of the action when an officer came from the *Victory* to tell me he was wounded. Horatio sent his love to me and desired me to conduct the fleet [Collingwood's version]. I asked the officer if the wound

was dangerous and he, by his look, told what he could not speak. I cannot now reflect upon that moment without suffering again the same anguish. You my dear madam, who know what our friendship was, can judge what I felt. All the praise and acclamations of joy for our victory, only bring to mind what it has cost.'

The circumstances did not allow Collingwood to grieve for there was work to be done. He never had the least doubt that the Royal Navy would triumph but he visualised himself, alongside Nelson, accepting the surrender and negotiating a favourable peace declaration. After the mess of warfare came the administration. Endless letters and reports would flow from the bloody events of this day and Cuthbert Collingwood would have to do it alone; the burden of responsibility had fallen upon his solitary shoulders. He received, with a heavy heart; the first incomplete list of killed and wounded which showed the death of 21 officers, 16 petty officers, 299 seamen and 113 marines - 449 bereavement letters to be written. The seriously wounded and incapacitated revealed 43 officers, 59 petty officers 900 seamen and 212 marines. In the days that followed there would be many more additions to this harrowing roll call.

Collingwood's first task after the battle was to transfer his blue flag (as Rear-Admiral of the Blue) to the *Euryalus*. The *Royal Sovereign* had taken such a battering that it had to be taken in tow. Choosing *Euryalus* was a deserved compliment to Captain Blackwood whose signal staff did excellent work and it was from this frigate that Collingwood wrote the dispatch which inspired and saddened his countrymen. This was published and made known to the public in The Times on Thursday 7th November 1805 - seventeen days after the event. In the dispatch, dated 22nd October, the day following the conflict, he issued what was known as a 'General Order' and in this Collingwood broke with tradition. The conventional declaration normally highlighted the success of a battle and as a postscript mentions the dead and wounded. In the case of Trafalgar, Collingwood put his friend at the forefront of the report and his moving, eloquent words perpetuated the heroism of Horatio and added to the legend. It was a fitting tribute to the men, whatever their rank, who fought on that momentous day. The new commander demonstrated a generosity of spirit and declined, modestly, to comment on his own vital contribution. Collingwood, only hours after the terrible struggle, wrote from the heart to tell the country of the glorious triumph and the loss of a beloved hero:

'*Euryalus*, off Cape Trafalgar, 22nd October 1805
The ever-to-be lamented death of Lord Viscount Nelson, Duke of Bronte, the Commander-in-Chief, who fell in the action of the 21st, in the arms of *Victory*, covered with glory - whose name will be ever dear to the British Navy and the British Nation, whose zeal for the honour of his King, and for the interest of his Country, will be ever held up as a shining example for a British seaman - leaves me a duty to return my thanks to the Right Honourable Rear-Admiral, the Captains, Officers, Seamen and Detachments

of Royal marines, serving on board His Majesty's squadron, now under my command, for their conduct on the day; but where can I find the language to express my sentiments of the valour and skill which was displayed by the Officers, the Seamen and Marines, in the battle with the enemy, where every individual appeared a hero on whom the glory of his Country depended? The attack was irresistible, and the issue of it adds to the page of naval annals a brilliant instance of what Britons can do, when their King and Country need their service.'

Collingwood's report appeared in The Times seventeen days after the event

At the time of writing, the sea was turbulent and the expected storm was blowing up. Collingwood had hoped to set aside a day of praise and thanksgiving to God, as was customary, but he added a postscript:

'NB The fleet has been dispersed by a gale of wind, no day has yet been able to be appointed for the above purpose.'

The wind that Collingwood described, raged relentlessly. Storm, heavy rain and all-obscuring nimbus clouds followed; for four days and nights neither sun, moon, nor stars were seen. With the benefit of hindsight, Nelson's supporters believe that Collingwood should have carried out the Commander-in-Chief's final order, which was to anchor. Collingwood was well aware of the danger and he had hoped to gather the enemy prizes, all fourteen of them, into Cadiz. The expected gale came up from the south-west and those ships that could anchor, did so, but many vessels had lost the necessary tackle; including the *Victory* and the *Royal Sovereign* - both were de-masted and in tow. All the ships had been ravaged by gunfire twelve hours earlier and mutilated bodies still lay on the decks. Every able-bodied survivor would have been exhausted after the exertions of battle and it was reported that the captured enemy were 'demoralised and broken in spirit'. It was a cruel blow to have to contend with a storm of such violence that would see them fighting once again for their lives - against an unpredictable foe.

Collingwood alone had to deal with the crisis and call on his diminishing reserves of strength. He had no second in command, no one to consult with or to offer advice, and he had an immediate decision to make. The new Commander-in-Chief considered that it would be less damaging for the fleet to stand off the wind to the westward in the open sea. The experienced Northumbrian could judge the prevailing conditions better than any seamen but inevitably there were many who believe that he took the wrong option. Entries in ships' log books at the time of the storm read:

> 'Fleet and prizes much scattered.. lost three hawsers and 100 fathoms of rope towing prizes *L'Aigle* and *Fougueux*. *Redoubtable* was rolling so violently, she carried away her foremast - the only mast she had standing. *Neptune* is foundering and is beyond help.'

At the outset of the battle, both Nelson and his second-in-command had sought annihilation of the enemy. The captured prizes were an added bonus - a financial reward to all the survivors who participated in the victory. Had the weather been favourable, all fourteen ships would have been brought into a safe haven. They would have been repaired and added to the existing warships to strengthen the British fleet - the vessels, battered but floating, were unquestionably a prize asset. However, in these hours of crisis, Collingwood feared that the enemy ships might be scattered and escape and he had already heard that there was some resistance in several of the defeated vessels. When the enemy ships first surrendered, British seaman and marines boarded at the earliest opportunity to guard their prizes and to bring them to safety. After the devastation of battle, available men were thin on the ground and they were clearly unable to handle the passage to port of the fourteen damaged hulks.

On the 24th October, three days after the battle and with the weather still furious, Collingwood took the deeply unpopular decision to destroy many of the captive vessels. His signal was 'Quit and withdraw men from prizes after having destroyed or disabled them.' The men were ordered to remove prisoners and vacate the ships then sink them or destroy the vessels with explosives. It was a sad moment for the fleet and afterwards Collingwood admitted:

> 'I can only say that in my life, I would rather fight another battle, than pass such a week as the one that followed.'

It was an unprecedented responsibility for one man and whilst his fleet knew in their heart of hearts that their commander was right, there was no immediate joy after the triumph of battle. Officers and men were robbed of the visible signs of their triumph; still more important to them, they saw their prize money vanish beneath the waves. There was even more misery as four of the captured ships could not be controlled in the storm. The heavy waves swept them onto the deadly rocky shore and tragically, they were wrecked with all hands. It is difficult to appreciate the wretched

A French ship is wrecked in the storm

state of these poor souls who had overcome the cannons only to be taken by the elements.

The enemy ship that every man in the Royal Navy wanted to see back in England was the *Santissima Trinidada* - the mighty talisman of the Spanish fleet. Lieutenant Edwards of the *Prince* described the fate of the superb man-o'-war:

> 'We had the *Trinidada* in tow, the largest ship in the world. 'Tis impossible to describe the horrors the morning presented, nothing but signals of distress flying in every direction. The signal was made to destroy the prizes. We had no time before to remove the prisoners; but what a sight when we came to remove the wounded, of which there were between three and four hundred. We had to tie the poor mangled wretches round their waists, and lower them down into a tumbling boat, some without arms, others no legs, and lacerated all over in the most dreadful manner.'

The *Santissima Trinidada* sank before the weary repair party could plug the holes below her water line. She had escaped once before at the battle of St Vincent but now there was no reprieve for the finest ship afloat. In view of the condition of the ships, after the hardest fought battle on record, it was doubtful if any more could have survived - even with anchorage. It was an unfortunate finale to Trafalgar and the outcome did not win Cuthbert Collingwood many friends. The Commander-in-Chief's official report stated:

> 'Only four of the prizes have been saved and towed into Gibraltar. I can only say that in my life I never saw such exertions as were made to save those ships.
>
> The storm being violent, and with many of our ships in a most perilous situations, I found it necessary to order the captures, all without masts, some without rudders, and many half full of water, to be destroyed, except such as were in better plight; for my object was their ruin and not what might be made of them. Nelson would have approved, for that was his sentiment.'

Collingwood reported a conversation he had had with a Spanish captain who found it difficult to believe that the English fleet remained intact - not one loss. The Northumbrian assured him and the Spaniard replied dejectedly:

> 'How can we contend with such people, on whom the utmost violence of the elements has no effect?'

Napoleon Bonaparte's official comment typically blamed Commander Villeneuve and did not acknowledge defeat:

> 'Gales have caused the loss of several vessels after a battle which had been entered upon imprudently.'

The fact remained that the British ships, which had also taken heavy punishment in the engagement, did not run ashore or founder - although many had a hard time in weathering the storm.

It is interesting to reflect on the various attitudes after the battle. Napoleon must have been bitterly disappointed for it meant that his Grand Army would now be disbanded and the planned invasion would not take place. His public declarations are few and naturally this setback does not loom large in French history. France was no different to other nations when it chose to celebrate victorious events and tended to disregard failure. The success for the Royal Navy was achieved

The demasting of the Santissima Trinidada

mainly by the skill and 'reward' motivation of the sailors and of course inspirational leadership. The combined enemy fleet lacked the sailing and gunnery experience and the wholesale slaughter of French naval officers during the revolution did not improve their chances. The enemy did have bigger and better ships but they could not match the manoeuvrability and fire-power of the British.

Another major factor was that the Royal Navy leaders fought from the front and this was not something that happened in conventional land warfare where the battles were directed at a safe distance behind the front line. The French and the Spanish thought Nelson was reckless, not only for his unorthodox methods, but for making himself so visible in the firing line and they felt, in the end, he got what he deserved. Whilst this tactic may have inspired the men - as did the cool confidence of Collingwood munching an apple on the quarter deck during the heat of battle - it certainly does seem foolhardy. Nelson of course was removed from Trafalgar very early on and although he died a hero, it could be argued his death was needless. Should he not have been under cover or had some sort of protective shield? His value to the Royal Navy was immeasurable yet he was conspicuously dressed in his medals and almost invited fire from the enemy marines. Horatio had a sense of destiny and he wrote many times that he believed God was watching over him personally and that his Maker would choose the time and place. It was a high-risk faith. Collingwood shared a similar belief to his friend and he too faced the enemy exchanges with what appears to be equanimity. Although it was not widely reported, Collingwood was injured in the battle with severe bruises on his back and shoulder, cuts on his face and deep lacerations on his legs. His wounds horrified a Spanish captain who was taken on board his ship but the Northumbrian Vice-Admiral made light of them and did not refer to his injuries in his letters home, perhaps out of consideration to his family.

In the event, Collingwood survived but he could easily have been killed in action. What then? Were there contingency plans for a third in command to take over control of the battle? There must have been some arrangement but without Nelson or Collingwood's leadership would we still have won? It seems extraordinary that the fate of the nation depended on the survival of these two admirals yet they were both so unwisely exposed. The British nation ought to be extremely grateful that Collingwood was fortunate to live through the bombardments and finish the job he started.

When prize money and grants were distributed, there were five classes of share.
The highest payment...... £3,362.7.6d [2005 value = £340,000] Admirals.
Second class...................... 225.11s [2005 = £22,500] Captains.
Third and Fourth class.. £148.12s [2005 = £15,000] Officers.
Fifth Class......................... £27 [2005 = £2,700] Midshipmen and Able
                                              Seamen.
Ordinary seaman.............. £6.10s [2005 = £650] Rank and file.
For the injured, the Committee of Lloyds, added sums for:
Severely wounded lieutenants......... £100 [2005 = £10,000]
For slightly wounded seamen......... £10 [2005 =£1,000]

Prize was one thing; credit another. The share-out, although not insubstantial, (at least for the officers and skilled seamen) was received with a grudging what-might-have-been acceptance. Cuthbert Collingwood did not express regret or sympathy for the reduced prize money, he simply presented the figures as a fait accompli. At this time the weight of responsibility lay heavily on his shoulders but Collingwood, tired as he was by the events of the battle and the storm which followed, never for one moment lost his grip of the strategic as well as tactical situation. He never relaxed, never tolerated negligence in his captains, and tirelessly sought to tie up the loose ends of the wider campaign that had to be attended to. Collingwood's assessment of the outcome was forthright:

> 'I will venture to say that had this battle been fought on the ocean, far from land and unembarrassed by the rocks and shoals of Gibraltar, not one of the enemy ships would have been allowed to escape. As soon as I can make the necessary arrangements, I propose going into the Mediterranean and if the Spanish squadron off Carthegena is in motion and at sea, to use my utmost endeavours to destroy them also and send to the Italian coast such a force as will check any operations the enemy may have in contemplation.'

The recent memory of the horror of warfare did not for one moment deter Collingwood from finishing off the job. The British may have lost no ships but nearly 1,700 men had been killed or wounded. The combined French and Spanish fleets had lost eighteen ships and nearly 6,000 men killed or wounded and 20,000 taken prisoner. It was not total annihilation but it was total victory. The Royal Navy had taken command of the seas once more and Collingwood had the whole management of the fleet, a task that would occupy him continuously over the next five years.

Meanwhile the lifeless Lord Nelson was not thrown overboard, unlike most of his crew. His hair was cut off, and, dressed only in a shirt, was preserved in a cask, or barrel that was known as a leaguer. Brandy was poured in to prevent decay and his corpse remained on the *Victory*, which was towed to Gibraltar. Here, his body was transferred to a lead coffin and filled with spirits of wine, a better preservative. And the brandy? Some of his men were allowed to drink it in honour of their commander! A schooner (appropriately named the *Pickle*) was sent to England with the triumphant Trafalgar dispatches and the sad news that Lord Nelson was on his way home.

It was early in December 1805 when the *Victory* was towed to Greenwich Hospital with Nelson's coffin. The heroic lord lay in state for three days before being placed on a barge that was rowed up the River Thames by some of his sailors, as silent crowds watched from the riverbanks. His body was led by 10,000 troops through the streets of London where it was said that the only sound, as the procession passed, was the rustle of the roadside mourners who were removing their hats. His final resting place was in St Paul's Cathedral, where Nelson had asked to be buried.

Nelson's funeral barge being rowed up the River Thames

Admiral Villeneuve, the captured French leader, witnessed the funeral of Lord Nelson in London; Collingwood and his senior officers were not permitted to attend. Afterwards Villeneuve was allowed to leave England for his homeland. He had been taken on board the *Euryalus* after the battle and Collingwood had spent time with him. The meetings were cordial and although Villeneuve was low in spirits he was 'gentlemanlike' and, according to Collingwood's letter home, 'acknowledged, with due courtesy, that his fleet were no match for the British at sea.' In spite of the enmity between them, Collingwood and Villeneuve clearly shared a mutual regard and respect for each other's abilities and experiences. The French Admiral, on his return to his homeland, remained grief-stricken and shortly afterwards he took his own life.

Lord Nelson's last request: 'Take care of poor Lady Hamilton and Horatia' was ignored. Whilst the nation was happy to celebrate the heroic victory, they turned their own blind eye to his wishes - Emma was not even allowed to attend the funeral. The main beneficiaries of Nelson's death were his sisters who received £10,000 each and Fanny his estranged wife who received a £2,000 annual pension. It was his clergyman brother who received the lion share. William acquired all his brother's titles, received an earldom and £90,000 [2005 = £10m] from public donations, and an annuity of £5,000. Collingwood knew William from his days when he served as a chaplain in the West Indies (the cleric could not cope with the post or the climate and returned home prematurely) and the Vice-Admiral described him with uncharacteristic vituperation:

> 'I suppose all the public money will go to the parson, who of all the dull, stupid fellows you ever saw, he is the most so. There is nothing in him like a gentleman and he was never intended for anything superior than village curate. Yet he has, by Nature's frisk, been raised to the highest dignity, without his body and mind having anything to do with it. He has bestowed upon himself the title Earl Nelson of Trafalgar and Merton; all for having a heroic brother.'

As for Lady Hamilton, she received nothing and neither did their illegitimate daughter. Emma was an embarrassment and the authorities did not want to be reminded of their hero's infidelity, in spite of his dying plea. In 1815, Lady Hamilton would die in Calais, an alcoholic, after spending time in a debtor's prison. It seems that Horatia had also disowned her memory, for she would eventually marry a vicar, have nine children and live to the ripe old age of 81. She was proud to tell the world about her illustrious father, but she never admitted that Emma was her mother.

Horatia Nelson

When the storm eventually dispersed Collingwood counted the cost. At the outset of the battle there had been 33 enemy war-ships - 18 French and 15 Spanish. After the fighting and the gales, only four ships were brought into Gibraltar as prizes - three Spanish, one French. Sixteen ships sank and others were burnt or wrecked beyond recovery. In the aftermath of the ferocious battle and terrible storm, Collingwood had done all in his power to rescue as many of his prisoners as possible. Once the surrender was complete he had shared a mutual sympathy with vanquished sailors and his own men risked their lives in ferrying the defeated seamen from their stricken ships. Collingwood generously transported the enemy wounded back to the shore and this compassionate gesture was appreciated by Spain. It had been an intuitive act of mercy and Collingwood would report:

> 'Nothing can exceed the gratitude expressed by Marquis Solana for this act of humanity. All in this part of Spain is in uproar of praise and thankfulness to the English.'

Solana had sent Collingwood a cask of wine and offered his hospitals for the

British wounded, pledging Spain's honour for their care. After the recent animosity in battle, there now seemed to be a gentleman's agreement between Spain and Britain. Collingwood appreciated the Spanish hand of friendship:

> 'Our officers and men who were wrecked in some of their prize ships were received on the beaches where priests and women distributed wine and bread and fruit. Soldiers were turned out of their barracks to make lodgings for our people.'

Conversely the French survivors, supposedly Spain's allies, were not treated well by the Spanish and a guard was placed over them.

One of Collingwood's earliest tasks was to replace and promote a number of officers. He wrote personally to Admiral Sir Peter Parker, who had given both Nelson and himself their command opportunities 25 years earlier in the West Indies:

> 'You will have seen from the public accounts that we have fought a great battle and that two of your own pupils, raised under your eye, and cherished by your kindness, should render such service to their country. I have made advantages of our calamities, and having lost two excellent men [Captains Duff and Cooke] I have endeavoured to replace them with those who will in due time, I hope, be as good. I have appointed Captain Parker to the *Melphomene*, which, I am sure my dear Nelson would have done had he lived. His own merit entitles him to it, and it is highly gratifying for me to give you such a token of my affection to you.'

Captain Parker was the old man's grandson and the promotion, which as Collingwood justified, was nevertheless a personal mark of appreciation for the confidence he had shown a quarter of a century earlier in raising two young seamen from lieutenants to post captains. In fact, Collingwood was generous to all who had participated in the battle and when Captain Blackwood of the *Euryalus* hinted that certain ships had not pulled their weight, the Northumbrian was very firm:

> 'Sir, this has been a glorious victory for England and for Europe - don't let there be a reflection against even the humblest cabin boy.'

Collingwood wrote several accounts of the Battle of Trafalgar to various authorities and all are remarkable considering they were composed in the cramped quarters of a warship that was tossing about on the ocean. As the Commander-in-Chief he was obliged to send letters and dispatches to the Admiralty and he had to deal with a constant stream of important information. Collingwood

King George III

responded to reports that were continually being received and he had to make vital decisions hour by hour. Signals needed to be sent to the fleet and he had, without warning, the whole complicated Mediterranean strategy and diplomacy suddenly thrust upon him. Collingwood had just spent months on watch in all weathers; he had fought in the greatest of sea battles, lost his closest friend and many serving officers. He was approaching sixty and yet, single-handedly, he was able to pull all the elements together. Collingwood had not sought such a position of responsibility but the affairs of the nation could not have been in safer hands. It is a measure of the Government's confidence that they relied on Collingwood as both admiral and ambassador. The King, who did not know Cuthbert personally, placed unwavering trust in the Northumbrian for the rest of his naval life. The Secretary of the Admiralty wrote to Collingwood after being instructed to by George III:

Windsor, 7th November 1805

'His Majesty has commanded me to express, in the strongest terms, his feelings of approbation of every part of the conduct of his gallant Fleet, whose glorious and meritorious exertions are made yet more conspicuous, if possible, by the details of the opposition and difficulties which it had to encounter, both during and subsequent to the glorious action, and by the intrepidity and skill with which they were overcome.

Every tribute of praise appears to His Majesty due to Lord Nelson, whose loss he can never sufficiently regret; but His Majesty considers it very fortunate that the command, under circumstances so critical, should have devolved upon an officer of such consummate valour, judgement and skill, as Admiral Collingwood has proved himself to be, every part of whose conduct he considers deserving his entire approbation and admiration. The feeling manner in which he has described the events of that great day and those subsequent, and the modesty with which he speaks of himself, whilst he does justice, in terms so elegant and so ample, to the meritorious exertions of the gallant officers and men under his command, have also proved extremely satisfactory to the King.'

Collingwood regarded this as his most prized possession. There is family pride in the royal correspondence but typically, in a note to his sister, we also see the Collingwood modesty:

'Show it to anybody, that it may be publicly known of what His Majesty's opinion of my services is, but allow no one to have a copy of it, lest it should get into a newspaper.'

On Christmas Day 1805, when Cuthbert was relentlessly patrolling at sea, he wrote to Sarah and said of the King's letter: 'I feel that the object of my life is attained.'

After he had dealt with the most pressing administrative correspondence Collingwood allowed himself to reflect on the loss of his friend. The business surrounding 'Trafalgar' had kept his mind active but in his quieter moments he expressed his true feelings. In a letter to Blackett he wrote:

'When my dear friend received his wound, he immediately sent an officer to me to tell me of it, and give his love to me. Though the officer was directed to say the wound was not dangerous, I read in his countenance what I had to fear; and before the action was over, Captain Hardy came to inform me of his death. I cannot tell you how deeply I was affected; my friendship for him was unlike anything I have left in the Navy - a brotherhood of more than thirty years. In this affair he did nothing without my counsel, we made our line of battle together, and concerted the mode of attack, which was put in execution in the most admirable style.'

Their collaboration has never been widely known, nor acknowledged.

In a letter to W. Spencer-Stanley he added:

'Since the year '73 we had been on the terms of greatest intimacy; chance had thrown us very much together in service, and on many occasions we acted in concert; there is scarce a naval subject that has not entered our discussion, so that his opinions were familiar to me, and so entirely founded on principles of honour, of justice, of attachment to his country. He liked fame, and was open to flattery, so that people got about him who were unworthy of him: he is a loss to his country that cannot easily be replaced.'

Death of Nelson

102

LORD COLLINGWOOD

Commander-in-Chief

To add something more to this wonderful year.

Collingwood was soon to receive the thanks of both Houses of Parliament and they made him a peer of the realm as Baron Collingwood of Caldburne and Hethpool, named after his properties in the upper reaches of Northumberland. He was permitted to add a lion of England to his family coat of arms with the words 'Trafalgar' above it. The stern of the *Royal Sovereign* was also added as a crest to his insignia. Collingwood received the freedom of many cities and was granted a substantial pension of £2,000 per annum which reduced to £1,000 for his wife Sarah on his death. His daughters each received £500 annually but a request that his peerage should pass through his daughters was not acted upon - much to his regret. As the awards were bestowed he told Sarah that his constant companion Bounce, was getting above himself:

> 'The consequential airs he gives himself since he became a right honourable dog are insufferable. He considers it beneath his dignity to play with commoner's dogs, and truly thinks that he does them grace when he condescends to lift up his leg against them. This, I think, is carrying the insolence of rank to the extreme, but he is a dog that does it.'

Collingwood was promoted to Vice-Admiral of the Red, which took him past the highest rank that Nelson ever achieved and by the time of his death he was Commander-in-Chief in the Mediterranean and held the second highest rank in the Royal Navy.

By the end of 1805 Cuthbert was still overworked but was comforted by the belief that eventually he would be returning home. There is deep affection and nostalgia for his family and garden and this is evident in his letter to Sarah:

> 'I labour from dawn till midnight, till I can hardly see; and as my hearing fails me too, you will have but a mass of infirmities in your poor Lord whenever he returns to you. I shall not be able to work in my garden now; but tell old Scott that he need not be unhappy on that account. I shall not be able to plant the Nelson potatoes, but we will have some other sort and some right noble cabbages to boot, in great perfection.'

The thought of his garden plot lifted his spirits but a fortnight later he was writing again to Blackett with less certainty:

> 'It was once full in the contemplation of my mind, considering that I am now far in advanced years, to have retired from sea service when my three

years were up, in May next; but I am afraid that is now out of the question and as long as I have health I must go on.'

Collingwood was unable to assist with the affairs of his family from such a distance and although his children were attending school and approaching their teens he could only offer advice and instructions through his correspondence, which he did with increasing regularity. He was a fervent Tynesider yet he saw the disadvantage of a strong regional accent, which he felt might make his children appear uncouth. He believed that speech was important but it was not, he maintained, the most overriding quality:

'Their hearts and their minds, are of much more consequence than their tongues.'

He had been looking forward to returning home and instilling some of the wisdom and learning that he wished them to acquire but in the meantime he could send instructions:

'I would like the girls to be taught mathematics and geometry - of all sciences in the world these are the most entertaining. Also astronomy to give them an idea of the beauty and wonder of creation so they may have a fixed idea of the nature of that Being who could be the author of such a world. Whenever they have that, nothing on this side of the moon will give them uneasiness of mind.'

Collingwood had learnt French and he encouraged his wife to see that his daughter Sarah learnt the language although his comments on the nation were caustic:

'The language is the only thing French she need possess for there is very little else from that country which I should wish her to love or imitate.'

He was always concerned that his girls should be brought up correctly and when Sarah and Mary Patience were twelve and eleven respectively, he declared his literary preferences to his father-in-law:

'I am delighted with your account of my children's improvement, for it is a subject of the greatest anxiety to me. Above all things, keep novels out of their reach. They are corrupters of tender minds: they exercise the imagination instead of the judgement and make them all desire to become the Julias and Cecilias of romance. Novels turn their heads before they are enabled to distinguish truth from these fictions which are devised merely for entertainment. When they have passed their climacteric it will be time enough to begin novels.'

A 'climacteric', according to the Oxford English Dictionary is a 'period of life when fertility and sexual activity are in decline' in other words, when they are old maids!

It is understandable that Cuthbert Collingwood, lover of Shakespeare and the classics, should have been repelled by the novels of his day which were trivial and frivolous. What this pious parent could not have known, was that one of his fellow officers, the highly regarded Captain Francis Austen - close friend of

Nelson - had a sister who was making her mark as an author. It was Jane Austen who would transform the novel into an art form with her wit and social observation, and it was she who brought about the change in the Georgian and Victorian literary landscape. Collingwood, a lover of good literature, would certainly have approved of the sense and sensibility of the novelist, whose books would be highly suitable reading matter for his daughters. The ex-Newcastle Royal Grammar School pupil may appear at times to be rather stuffy and censorious in his letters but there is abundant evidence of a wry humour, sharp insight and clarity of thought - all qualities that Miss Austen embraced.

Jane Austen

Cuthbert's wife, Sarah, enjoyed entertainment and having such a celebrated husband ensured that there were few gaps in her social diary. The demand for the appearance of Lady Collingwood spread beyond her native North East and the capital city desired her presence. In Cuthbert's letter dated 5th April 1806 he comments on the family's visit to London where Sarah is to be presented at Court. His daughters are also travelling to the capital and he is anxious that they make the most of the experience:

'I hope that in this journey the education of our children does not stop; but that, even on the road, they may study the geography of that part of England through which they travel, and keep a regular journal, not of what they eat and drink but of the nature of the country, its appearance, its produce, and some gay description of the manners of the inhabitants. I hope you will take your time in town and show my girls everything curious. I am sure you will visit the tomb of my dear friend. Alas! The day that he had a tomb.'

Collingwood was of course referring to the sarcophagus in the crypt of St Paul's Cathedral - a location which would be the Northumbrian's own final resting place.

At around this time, the Vice-Admiral heard from home that his cousin, Edward John Collingwood, had unexpectedly died and that he was to inherit the property of the deceased. Cuthbert was bequeathed the large estate at Chirton, near North Shields and close to the River Tyne, which included a working colliery. Collingwood was unable to return home to inspect his windfall and he had to undergo a detailed and lengthy correspondence before claiming ownership. He was obliged to write to the Duke of Northumberland, as there was an issue of access to the mine workings from the Duke's land. This was amicably resolved and the Duke, who had taken part in military campaigns, including the War of American Independence where Collingwood was first raised to officer rank. He

Chirton 1856

began a correspondence with Cuthbert and even asked if the Commander-in-Chief of the Mediterranean might help 'connect' some young friends into the Navy. Collingwood was used to these frequent requests and admitted to Sarah 'when I was the Captain of a frigate I took care of the boys; now I can not, and have not the time to know anything about them.' His constant administrative duties seemed to isolate him more than ever from his crew so that Bounce was his only confidant.

The 16th June 1806 was the fifteenth wedding anniversary of the Collingwood's and he wrote to Sarah telling her how much he missed his family. He suspected that Sarah might wish to set up the Collingwood home on the newly acquired Chirton Estate, and he was right. Cuthbert confessed that he had 'no desire to live near the proximity of collieries, with their noise, pumping engines and smoke'. From a distant shore, he tried dissuading his wife:

'If we leave Morpeth I should be for ever be regretting those beautiful views which are nowhere to be exceeded; and even the rattling of that old wagon at six o'clock on a winter's morning had its charms. The fact is, whenever I think of how I am to be happy again, my thoughts carry me back to Morpeth, where, out of the fuss and parade of the world surrounded by those I loved most dearly and who loved me, I enjoyed as much happiness as my nature is capable of.'

Cuthbert must have felt extremely low in spirits for he added:

'Is your sister with you, and is she well and happy? I wish I were with you, that we might have a good laugh. God bless me! I have scarcely laughed these three years.'

106

Sarah believed that their house at Morpeth, in spite of its happy associations, was not a suitable accommodation for a peer of the realm. The victorious Vice-Admiral who was used to the relatively simple life at sea, must have felt he was losing the domestic battle on the home front. He admitted to his brother:

'Chirton is a place I should dislike exceedingly as a residence. I could never bring my mind to be at home there. Yet it has more conveniences than Morpeth, and is more like a gentleman's house, but as it is, I fancy I must make Chirton my home in a very disagreeable neighbourhood with the smoke of coal engines and every kind of filth.'

His sister wrote to him and spoke of her stay at Morpeth - that stirred his emotions once again:

'How you delight me, my sister, when you speak of the comforts of my house and the beauties of my garden etc. I may say they are the work of my own hands. I planned everything and planted almost every tree, every honeysuckle and rose bush; the sturdy oak and tall poplar owe their stations to me. But how are the oaks; is there shade under them for a comfortable summer seat? Since Sarah has resolved for Chirton, she has cunningly left off talking of those old beauties of Morpeth.'

The discussion of their future residence was academic because Collingwood was not returning to England. There had been a rumour circulating that he was to be sent home but the Vice-Admiral commented that it probably arose from 'someone wishing to succeed my command.' He told Lord Radstock:

'I have heard from all quarters that I was going home, except from the Admiralty: Yet still Lord Howick invites me to continue my correspondence in matters relating to the political state of affairs.'

In England, their Lordships had little experience or knowledge of the situation in the Mediterranean and the government increasingly depended on Collingwood's assessment of a volatile continent. Collingwood knew his worth as a political adviser and he undoubtedly enjoyed his status as an important naval representative on the European stage. He was famous for not delegating and he believed (quite rightly) that no one in the British Fleet had his insight or expertise. Whilst the lure of retirement was very real he was unwilling to hand over the authority to a second-rate commander at this sensitive period. He put it succinctly in a festive letter which he wrote to Sarah off Cadiz on 20th December 1806:

'This is my second Christmas at sea and, unless it shall please God to take the Corsican [Napoleon] out of this out of this world, I see no prospect of a change.'

There were no more major sea battles after Trafalgar, although Collingwood and the Admiralty felt that there would be further action. The Vice-Admiral occupied the *Ocean*, a brand-new three-deck warship that accommodated 800 men. The perpetual motion of the vessel at sea meant that the enemy did not know her whereabouts for she did not anchor in port. As the principal flag ship, Collingwood had the best available officers and he sympathised with his zealous crew for he knew that they had 'the dullest life that can be conceived, and nothing but the utmost patience could endure it.'

Collingwood was apt to overemphasise the tedium for there was entertainment on board, which he encouraged, and this was provided by the crew for their own amusement. Every Thursday there would be an assembly and a concert or performance of a play. Cuthbert described an event in a letter to Sarah:

'We have an exceedingly good company of comedians, some dancers that might exhibit at an opera, and probably have done so at Sadlers Wells, and a band consisting of twelve very fine performers. Every Thursday is a play night, and they act as well as your Newcastle company.'

He describes how a visitor, the Governor of the province of Tetuan, was invited to the ship's entertainment and he had been astonished at the good behaviour of the large audience. But it had been the performances of the male 'actresses' that captivated him:

'When the music began he was enchanted; but during the acting he was so transported with delight, that he could not keep his seat. His admiration for the ladies was quite ridiculous; and he is fully convinced that we carry female players to sea for the entertainment of the sailors: for though he could not find the ladies afterwards, he is not convinced that they are not put into some snug place till the next play-night.'

Collingwood had always encouraged entertainments among the sailors and he felt, quite rightly, that the distractions and a break from the routine were good for the ship's morale. The collective pleasure at bringing the men together helped lift spirits and the Thursdays were a highlight of the week.

By now, Napoleon had introduced his 'Continental System' which prevented nations from trading with the British Isles. Smuggling at this time was rife and although the British government retaliated by refusing to trade with the French, the attempted blockading on both sides was largely ineffective. The French troops were equipped with items made in England and Louis Bonaparte claimed 'you might as well try to stop the skin from sweating as to prevent trade.' Nevertheless, preventing supplies reaching Turkey was part of the Vice-Admiral's brief and it proved a difficult task. It added to the many jobs that the Commander-in-Chief had to deal with as he explained in letters home:

'My days are of constant labour, and with such a compound of subjects that really my head is sometimes giddy with them. The only pleasure I receive is the satisfaction that I have spared nothing to execute my trust faithfully.'

His mind remained sharp but his body was becoming weaker and by the summer of 1807 he assessed his physical condition:

'My eyes are weak, my body swollen, and my legs shrunk to tapers; but they serve my turn, for I have not much walking. I hardly ever see the face of an officer, except when they dine with me, and I am seldom on deck above an hour in the day, when I go in the twilight to breathe the fresh air.'

Collingwood had been incessantly cruising since Trafalgar and this maintained Britain's naval supremacy on the ocean but in mainland Europe he had no influence. Two years after the sea battle Cuthbert saw his fears realised. He had long since believed that the two European superpowers of France and Russia would join forces, and they did. The combination of the Tsar with Napoleon was an extremely threatening prospect, for, as the French Emperor claimed 'we shall parcel the world between us.' With the East in safe Russian hands, Napoleon could turn his attention to Portugal who had held out against France and was trading with Britain. Once the Portuguese were subdued this would bring Bonaparte closer to Spain and then the remaining obstacle would be 'that most obdurate enemy', Britain. There was no doubt in Collingwood's mind that the invasion of England remained the ultimate aim of the French despot.

In spite of the dominance of France, Collingwood was happy to report that Britain was still held in high esteem. After a buffeting off Toulon, Collingwood decided to put into Syracuse, in Sicily, for a re-fit. He wrote to his children of the reception he received telling them:

'It was once a place of great note, where all the magnificence and arts known in the world flourished. The inhabitants have a great natural civility. The Nobility and Senate waited on me in my ship. Another day, came all the military; the next, the Vicar General, for the Bishop was absent, and a levee of thirty priests - all fat, portly-looking gentlemen. In short, nothing was wanting to show their great respect and regard for the English. The nobles gave me and the officers a ball and supper, the most elegant thing I ever saw, and the best conducted.'

Cuthbert was grateful for such a demonstration of friendship but he was, as ever, incorruptible. He would never be seduced or persuaded by offerings and gifts. He was very much his own man and although always courteous and a gentleman, no one could 'buy' his good opinion.

During his stay at Syracuse, Cuthbert had his portrait painted and sent the picture home to his family. He was pleased with the work which he felt was a 'dignified representation' of his character and it seems his colleagues all agreed that the artist had caught his likeness. Sarah, however, was shocked when she saw the image of her husband. In her eyes, Collingwood appeared to have had grown old and careworn, and she told him so. There is a hint of pique in Cuthbert's

The Syracuse painting

109

response to Sarah when he wrote home admitting that his inability to exercise had created a certain flabbiness around his chin, and that his lack of sunlight had created a certain pallor to his complexion, but as to looking old and careworn, he replied: 'I am!'

At the turn of 1808, Collingwood received a message that the 'French squadron had put to sea.' The report was false but it did indicate that preparations were being made, so Collingwood gathered around him fifteen ship-of-the-line vessels in readiness. By the middle of March, the French Commander, Ganteaume, took advantage of gales that had blown the British watchers away from the port of Toulon and he ventured into the open sea with ten warships - all of over 80 guns each. The largest ship in Collingwood's fleet was a mere 74-gunner but this was the moment the Royal Navy had been waiting for. Collingwood believed that another 'Trafalgar' would see off the enemy ships for years to come. He was fully prepared and wrote out a 'General Order' [battle instructions] to all his captains on the 23rd March for he was sure a conflict was imminent. The detailed memorandum outlined his method of attack which was based on many years of personal experience.

At Trafalgar, Collingwood had broken through the enemy line without sustaining much too damage but many ships in both columns suffered severely from the enemy guns whilst 'running down'. The 'raking' fire had had a deadly effect, as Nelson's *Victory* would have testified. By exposing the British ships' bows and sterns to the enemy they made themselves particularly vulnerable. The broadside fire, where the combatants were facing each other, was not quite so fearsome for the British sailors because they could fire back more rapidly even though the British fleet had smaller ships and fewer guns than the enemy. Collingwood still favoured the idea of two columns; one attacking the van and one the rear, but his recommendation was to 'come at the enemy on a close parallel course before tacking though the line'. The instructions were masterful in their simplicity and covered every attacking eventuality. It was a plan devised for this particular confrontation where the number of warships was equal and Collingwood was flexible enough to modify his plan in the event of changed circumstances. He sent the instructions well in advance so no one could accuse the commander of being unprepared.

Prior to Trafalgar, Horatio had brought his captains aboard the *Victory* and explained his battle plan with drawings and a glass of wine. This had been the 'Nelson touch' where, as Horatio put it, 'some shed tears, all approved. I inspired them with confidence.' This was not Collingwood's way. He was not showy or demonstrative but the men around him knew that there was no one in the Royal Navy who had more authority and experience. Collingwood was a leader with a steely sense of duty and a certainty in his ability.

The battle-hardened seaman, now in his 60th year, was as sharp and determined as he had ever been to annihilate the opposition. The Northumbrian had never known the bitter taste of defeat in wartime; his career was marked only with success. His much-missed friend, Nelson, through recklessness and misjudgement, had known personal failure, notably at Tenerife and Boulogne, where many lives were needlessly lost. Collingwood's record and his clear-sightedness under pressure made him the ideal commander in a head-to-head confrontation. The Admiralty had complete confidence in Collingwood for there was no better man in the service to defend the freedom of his nation. Sarah was aware of her husband's commitment to King and Country which he placed above the interest of himself and his family. He admitted:

> 'Our country requires that great exertions should be made to maintain its independence and its glory. You know, when I am in earnest on any subject, how truly I devote myself to it; and the first object of my life, and what my heart is most bent on (I hope you will excuse me) is the glory of my country. To stand a barrier between the ambition of France and the independence of England, is the first wish of my life; and in my death, I would rather that my body, if it were possible, should be added to the rampart, than trailed in useless pomp through an idle throng.'

It was clear that the French were not anxious to meet with the might of the Royal Navy and in the vast seas they managed to avoid a confrontation. It was said that Collingwood's pursuit added years to a man already prematurely old. He was extremely disappointed and the only comfort he could take from the chase was the fact that the enemy had gone to ground:

> 'The only satisfaction that I have is, that they have done nothing, for when they found there was a probability of being overtaken, they quitted the place immediately. It has made me quite crazy for I know that in England success is the only criterion by which people judge, and lack of a battle is reckoned a great crime.'

Collingwood sought success for the safety of the country - he was not seeking personal glory. He had served forty-eight years on Royal Navy warships whose sole aim was to defend the country and its interests. Collingwood hoped for a final showdown with the hated French; this would have been the consummation of his life at sea. There would have been no doubt in his mind that he would have led the fleet to a famous victory and it would have been a fitting end to his life of service. The Vice-Admiral could not have known there would never be another battle on the scale of 'Trafalgar'. That historic confrontation, so skilfully concluded by Collingwood, would be the last sea-conflict of its kind. There would be no more face-to-face gun battles in ships of wood and sail.

Meanwhile Napoleon Bonaparte, who had signed a treaty with Spain in October 1807, now decided to attack Portugal. The British Navy stood by her ally and removed the Portuguese Regent and his fleet to Brazil for safekeeping. The French Emperor then stirred up trouble in Spain by forcing both King Charles and his son Ferdinand to renounce their claim to the kingdom. Napoleon shocked his Spanish allies by imprisoning the royals and placing his brother Joseph Bonaparte on the Spanish throne. This was too much for the people. They rose up in indignation and this series of events created what was known as the 'Spanish ulcer'. The damage in Napoleon's relationship with Spain was terminal and it proved to be a major factor in the downfall of the French Empire.

Collingwood saw the advantage for Great Britain in all the French political manoeuvrings and he was not slow to encourage Spain's opposition to Napoleon. The imposed conditions by an outside dictator produced the opposite of what Bonaparte intended and both Spain and Portugal began a war of independence against their powerful neighbour. Often it is small incidents which influence major events, and Collingwood's humane action after Trafalgar had not been forgotten. He had not sought popularity for delivering Spain's wounded back to their country but this chivalrous action had increased Cuthbert's personal standing. Britain could not have had a better representative abroad as Collingwood was looked upon as a hero at Cadiz. To further consolidate the British desire for peace and friendship, Cuthbert finally visited the ancient city that he had, for so many weary years, watched from the Atlantic. He described his reception to young Sarah:

Collingwood had watched Cadiz through his night-glass

> 'I went on shore a few days ago and you cannot conceive how rejoiced the people were to see me. I was received with all military honours; but, besides this, all the inhabitants, at least 40,000 men and women, came to welcome me.'

The man from Tyneside had supper with the Governor and 'altogether the visit was a gala occasion.' Collingwood was anxious to discuss the volatile situation in Spain and he correctly surmised that the people of Spain, with their royal family under arrest, were not willing to ally themselves to France in the foreseeable future. The French ships stationed at Cadiz surrendered to Collingwood without bloodshed and this opened up the port as a safe harbour to the British fleet once more. The diplomatic success led Cuthbert to feel that all his tireless energy and work had not been in vain. This would have been a happy conclusion to his years of service; surely he could now come home for a well-deserved rest? He was still hankering for a head-to-head with the old enemy before hanging up his compass and this is clear in a letter to his sister:

> 'I have written to the Admiralty and requested that their Lordships allow me to return to England and recover my shaken body, which I think you will be glad to hear. If I can have but one little finishing touch at the Frenchmen before I come out it will be a glorious termination. The Spaniards are going on well but they have a great deal to do.'

Soon after, his concerned sister received further correspondence that must have disappointed her:

'My proposition that I return home has not been accepted. I have heard that the Ministers totally disapprove of this, particularly Mr Canning [Foreign Secretary] and Lord Mulgrave [First Lord of the Admiralty] plainly writes to me that in the present state of affairs there is a difficulty in finding a proper person to succeed me. In short, it appears to me that I shall not get to England yet.'

Collingwood had done his job too well. The Government were alarmed at the thought of him returning home and Lord Mulgrave, the only naval officer that was above him in rank, virtually pleaded with him and admitted there was no one who could 'supply all that would be lost to the service of the country by your absence.' If Collingwood was dismayed he did not say so publicly. Mulgrave told his Mediterranean Commander-in-Chief that 'in no instance have you failed to adopt the most judicious and best-concerted measures in the interests of your country.' The appeal to Collingwood's patriotism and sense of duty, struck home.

Sadly for Collingwood there was another reason that kept him from home. The Duke of Clarence had put forward an application to succeed the ailing Northumbrian but he was thought to be totally unsuited for the job even though his royal credentials gave him a just claim. In his memoirs after Collingwood's death, Lord Mulgrave explained how he persuaded his man to stay at the helm:

'Old Cuddy, as we always called Lord Collingwood, who had worked all his life with greater diligence for professional applause than any other man, was tickled with the compliment, and this, acting on his devotion to the Service, procured his assent when it was obvious to all around him that his broken health rendered him quite unfit to retain so great a command. He replied that if the good of the Service required that he should remain, he was content to wait and die at his post, for he felt his days were numbered, and this proved too true.'

So Collingwood took up his position at sea overlooking Toulon once more. He could have given himself a posting ashore but he chose the arduous but necessary vigil of watching and waiting. The French were building and repairing their fleet and Cuthbert scrutinised their movements, as fifteen ship-of-the-line were made available to him. If the enemy should leave their haven then Collingwood was ready to pounce.

After nearly fifty years at sea, the Northumbrian had served on the older warships until they had rotted but he had always been impressed with their design and sea-worthiness. His brand-new vessel the *Ocean* had taken a tremendous battering in gales and he commented that 'the ship is almost to pieces although she has not a speck of rotten timber in her.' The Admiralty were soon made aware of his views on current ship designers: 'If they persist in building these wall-sided ships, no power of art can keep them together.' At the time of writing two-year-old Isambard Kingdom Brunel, was discovering the delights of his Portsmouth birthplace and would, thirty-five years later, design an iron ship that would dispel all of Collingwood's fears for the future.

Meanwhile the battered state of his own flagship forced him into Malta for repairs and it was from here that he received a message from King George:

'His Majesty has been greatly pleased to appoint your Lordship to be Major General of the Marines.'

This further recognition was an acknowledgement that Collingwood's work as Commander-in-Chief had caused trade to flow in the Mediterranean and the smaller islands were flourishing. He was as informative as ever in his letter to Blackett:

'Malta is the most gossiping, gormandising place I have ever heard of. The merchants there, two years since, were very little men, for they could not extend their trade. Now, with ample protection given to their speculations, and with other nations participating, they have become extremely rich. I have heard that some of them have made a hundred thousand pounds and several from ten to fifteen thousand a year [2005 = millionaires]. The ladies, who have so lately emerged from the humblest duties of domestic industry, now vie with each other in all the shining finery of tassel and tinsel, and pass their nights in routs and revels. I saw just enough of it to know that it would not do for me. Neither my health nor my occupations were suited to it, and I declined all invitations.'

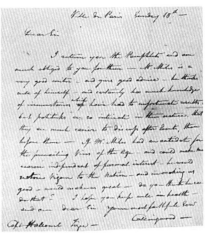

Collingwood correspondence

There was one visit that Collingwood felt obliged to make and that was to the Court of Palermo where Nelson had spent much of his time. It was necessary for Collingwood to play the ambassador as an act of courtesy and political expediency although from choice he had no wish to meet King Ferdinand and his Queen. As ever, Collingwood was prepared; he had brushed up his French (one of the languages of the Sicilian court) so that he could converse without an interpreter. His royal visit was a success although he found the King more like a country squire with his love of hunting and shooting on his estates. It was the Queen, he told his wife, that seemed to be the power behind the throne:

'She is a great politician and is continually engaged in intrigues for the recovery of her lost kingdom of Naples. The Queen would appear to be penetrating the soul and mind of every body that came near her. She would like to be thought of as a deep politician; yet all her schemes miscarry. She broods over what is impractical with her little means, and frets herself continually.'

Collingwood returned to the King where he found a patch of common ground:

'We dined with him on Sunday in his country house, and he carried us all over it. It is the prettiest thing that can be; the rooms are not larger than ours at Morpeth, and the house is not much bigger. We went over his grounds and gardens; and His Majesty seemed particularly desirous that I should see all his improvements, when I told him I was a great planter myself.'

He was not sorry to leave Sicily. Collingwood was unimpressed with the trappings of the rich. He was a simple man at heart and he embraced the Tyneside expression of 'I speak as I find'. He was ever the gentleman, and he always considered the feelings of others but underneath he was a man of sound common sense who was not influenced by outward show or the whims of fashion. He was not discourteous and appreciated the civilities of his hosts who were 'polite and attentive' but he was glad to be back on board his ship as he explained to Sarah:

'I have seen a great deal of Princesses and Duchesses of Sicily; and the more I see of them, I bless my stars that I was born in England, and have got a darling wife who is not a Princess.'

In April 1809 Collingwood moved into the *Ville de Paris* and he was very pleased to have a strong ship that sailed well; the *Ocean* was 'back almost to the state in which she was before her Malta repair.' He was happy to have the British-made, 120-gun vessel as his flag ship which had been the largest in the fleet when it was built in 1795. The ship was sound but the commander was not:

'Sarah, what I want most is a new pair of legs and a new pair of eyes; it is pretty clear that neither will last long. Tough as I am, I cannot last much longer. I have seen all the ships and men come and go two or three times. Many about me are yielding to the fatigue and confinement of a life which is certainly not natural to man. Bounce and I seem to be the only personages who stand our ground.'

His dog was a very affectionate companion who became a much-loved character on board his many ships. Bounce was attracted to everyone and everything - except explosions. Collingwood admitted:

'Bounce is my only pet now and he is indeed a good fellow: he sleeps by the side of my cot whenever I am in one. He slopes off whenever the ship is tacked because it usually means action, and he chooses to be out of hearing of the guns, for he has never been reconciled to them.'

Ville de Paris

As the years progressed, Bounce, like his master, became bored and overweight with inactivity. Collingwood echoed his own despondent predicament when he wrote that 'he sighs so piteously these long evenings.' Bounce was a remarkable companion to Cuthbert. He was continuously by his side and a great comfort to the lonely commander. Sadly, every dog has its proverbial day, and poor Bounce had had his, for on the 13th August, off Toulon, Collingwood wrote to his sister:

> 'You will be sorry to hear my poor dog Bounce is dead. I am afraid he fell overboard in the night. He is a great loss to me. I have few comforts, but he was one, for he loved me. Everybody sorrows for him. He was wiser than many of those who hold their heads higher, and was grateful to those who were kind to him.'

Bounce, like his master, had become old and worn out.

The loss of his companion coincided with news of difficulties from home. Sarah's management of the new house at Chirton seemed to be extremely costly and from a distance he was helpless to manage his affairs. Worse was to follow. His father-in-law had become involved in a 'fire office' insurance deal and Mr Blackett had invested £2,200 and used Collingwood's good name to stand surety for any loss. Collingwood was furious and he said so in a bitter letter home. He believed association with speculative business ventures was tarnishing his good name. Lord Collingwood felt that it was unseemly 'trade' and he was convinced that His Majesty would be 'unwilling to allow an insurance broker [himself] to sit in his house of peers.' Cuthbert was alarmed to think that his personal character might be 'established as a mercantile banker' (not the noblest of professions in the early 1800s) and he maintained that the shame he felt contributed to his illness and broken spirit.

His spirit was soon mended in the Mediterranean and his reputation was enhanced when, as the Major General in charge of the marines, he proposed sending 1,000 men to the Greek Ionian Islands. He had heard that the local population wished to see off the French influence there and Collingwood was happy to intervene. He had written to his superiors of his intentions but had not received their approval before acting. The timing was important and as Commander-in-Chief he took it upon himself to mount an offensive. The islanders were delighted with the support and protection from Britain as they liberated their territory from the French. It seems that Napoleon was preoccupied on the mainland but nevertheless it was a triumph for Lord Collingwood and the nation had gained a new friendly ally in Greece. He allowed himself a little pride when he informed Sarah:

> 'You will have great pleasure in hearing of my success, and particularly of its having been effected without a hair of any body's head being hurt, and almost without a shot being fired. I told the Admiralty what my plan was in September and it has succeeded to a marvel.'

By the end of 1809 Collingwood was very ill. He told his sister:

> 'The physician has much difficulty in determining the nature of my

complaint, which is in my stomach, and they say it is entirely the consequence of a sedentary life. I have lost digestion and have a constant pain, and my spirits are so low, that I am indifferent to everything.'

It seems likely that Cuthbert was suffering from pylorus; a condition which limits the movement of food from the stomach to the duodenum and his hours leaning over a cramped desk would certainly have been contributory. His diet and the anxiety of responsibility (which he was unwilling to share) could well have created an ulcer and it also seems probable that he was suffering from stomach cancer which only surgery could cure. He had bouts of melancholy but on the 1st January 1810 he wrote a friendly letter to his father-in-law and it would appear that his earlier anger had subsided:

'Thus the years roll on; and as the season comes round, I congratulate you, at the same time, on entering a new year of the world and of your life, which, I hope, you will enjoy in health, and pass in happiness.'

He went on to describe how one of the squadrons from his fleet had successfully attacked a French convoy and rather than be captured, the enemy had set fire to three of their ships, all 74-guns or more, and two of them had never been to sea before. The convoy was taken and Collingwood had dealt another blow to the French:

'In Sicily they are delighted; for whatever reduces the enemy's force diminishes their fears. I have a very handsome letter from the Prime Minister, who writes, in the King's name to congratulate me.'

In conclusion he told Mr Blackett that:

'Old age and infirmity are coming on very fast, and I am weak, and tottering on my legs.'

On the 22nd February, Collingwood finally admitted defeat - his failing body had outdone him. It was clear to himself and to all those around him, that he was no longer able to manage the command, so he resigned. He requested permission to return to England and explained to Lord Mulgrave:

'I am, at present, totally incapable of applying to the duties of my office. Since November I have received no benefit from medical advice; I am now almost unable to walk across my cabin; and as it is attributed to my long service in a ship, I have little hope of amendment until I can land.'

Collingwood pinned his hopes on time ashore at Port Mahon. It seems his doctor had recommended that he try gentle exercise on the back of a horse, but the Commander-in-Chief was incapable of coping with the slightest of movements. He was returned to the *Ville de Paris* and the ship set sail for England. On the morning of the 7th March there was considerable swell and his long-time friend, Captain Thomas, came into his cabin to ask if the motion was disturbing him. Collingwood replied:

'I am now in a state in which nothing in this world can disturb me more. I am dying; and I am sure it will be consolatory to you, and all who love me, to see how comfortably I am coming to my end.'

117

He was said to have spoken to one of his attendants and explained that he had attempted to review his past life and that he was happy to say that nothing had given him a moment's uneasiness. He spoke of his family and his country with a calmness and resignation. Collingwood's belief in God gave him peace of mind and as his son-in-law, Newnham Collingwood wrote:

'After taking an affectionate farewell of his attendants, he expired without a struggle at six o'clock in the evening of that day. Lord Collingwood's death was dignified and noble. He was cruelly harassed by a most afflicting disease, yet he met death with composure and fortitude.'

Cuthbert Collingwood died at the age of 61 years, 5 months and 8 days.

Trafalgar was a pivotal moment in the fortunes of the nation and Cuthbert Collingwood had been there to see the battle to its end. His arduous years of service before the event were necessary in the making of the man. The conclusion of the battle and the peace that followed was down to Collingwood's indefatigable leadership. In the 21st Century it is difficult to imagine any citizen putting the nation before their family but Cuthbert Collingwood did just that. The values of the Vice-Admiral demanded that duty to King and country was the first priority and he never wavered from that belief. He had spent only one year at home in the previous seventeen and only seven years in total from his fifty years of service. In the final period of his life he had the memory of his family and home to comfort him but it is difficult to imagine Collingwood resting easily when there was work to be done for the preservation and defence of England. He was never an easy man to work under. He drove himself relentlessly and expected his subordinates to be as committed. Much has been said of his icy persona and lack of warmth but these observations never came from the men who served under him. An ordinary seaman, Robert Hay, was fifteen years old when he was in the *Culloden* in 1804 when Collingwood was in command. It was a time, just prior to Trafalgar, when there was restlessness and inactivity amongst the fleet. The popularity of Collingwood, the Commander-in-Chief, was said to be at a low ebb. Not with his crew it seems, for Robert Hay paints a different picture:

'A better seaman - a better friend to seamen - a greater lover and more zealous defender of the country's rights and honour, never trod a quarterdeck. He and his favourite dog Bounce were known to every member of the crew. How attentive he was to the comfort and happiness of his crew! A man who could not be happy under him, could have been happy nowhere; a look of displeasure from him was as bad as a dozen at the gangway from another man.'

St Paul's Cathedral

Collingwood's body was brought to England and lay in Greenwich Hospital before making the journey overland to St Paul's Cathedral in London. Here, Lord Chancellor Eldon, his school companion from fifty years earlier, witnessed the interment of his fellow Northumbrian as his remains were placed alongside his heroic friend, Horatio Nelson. It was a sombre occasion and lacked the spectacle of five years earlier when the nation had turned out in their tens of thousands. In 1805 the Royal Navy had celebrated a great victory at sea and this was tempered by the death of Nelson who had touched the hearts of every citizen. Cuthbert Collingwood's death was low-key by contrast. He had died in his bed, having been desk-bound for many years, and his demise, no less in the service of his country, lacked the drama of a heat-of-the-battle conflict. Now, the island nation had become complacent and secure, thanks to Cuthbert Collingwood's tight control of the seas and the enemy ports. This allowed the military to increase in strength and it paved the way for Wellington's success at Waterloo five years later when Napoleon was finally defeated. Great Britain's shore was no longer threatened and its dominance of the sea would last for another hundred years.

The Northumbrian's final resting place, in the crypt close to Nelson

It is not fanciful to suggest that Collingwood's leadership, at a critical period, saved the nation from the clutches of a powerful enemy. It is also true that this man, trained for sea-warfare, would play a vital role as diplomat and politician in the highly combustible Mediterranean, where Collingwood ensured that stability was maintained and that British interests were safeguarded. He had no training for diplomacy but his strong sense of duty and intuitive response, based on half a century of service, guaranteed that the defence of his country was in safe hands. Against the grain, he was forced into physical inactivity as most of his years after Trafalgar were spent leaning over his desk in the daylight hours writing endless letters and reports. Collingwood's death was not spectacular, there was no bullet to send him to oblivion, just a painful lingering illness - not a fitting end for a hero. The Vice-Admiral would never claim special recognition, even after Trafalgar when the public were moved by his tribute to Lord Nelson which echoed the mood of the nation, Collingwood remained reticent and modest about his achievements. In response to an appeal for biographical notes he said:

> 'I find great difficulty in writing anything about myself that can be ever interesting or entertaining to the public. My life has been a continued service at sea, but unmarked by any of those extraordinary events, or

brilliant scenes, which hold men up to particular attention, and distinguish them from those officers who are zealous, and anxious for public service.'

It was left to others to acknowledge his personal qualities; there were many contemporary observers who were generous in their praise. Captain Henry Lockwood of the *Euryalus* which Vice-Admiral Collingwood transferred to when the *Royal Sovereign* was disabled, remarked:

'He was a reserved, though very pleasing good man, and as he fought like an angel, the more I take to him.'

Captain William Hoste was a protégé of Nelson, but he too, was quick to praise the Northumbrian:

'Never shall we find Nelson's equal... but Lord Collingwood is a different man and as brave an old boy as ever stood. There was no one who was better calculated for the general good of the service and no one who could have served his country better in the important overseas stations.'

But perhaps it was the non-seafaring thoughts of William Makepeace Thackeray, novelist and social commentator, which would have given the surviving Collingwood family great comfort. He had read the published correspondence of Vice-Admiral and felt compelled to write:

'I think since heaven made gentlemen, there can be no record of a better one. Where would you find a nobler, kinder, more beautiful life of duty, of a gentler truer heart? In reading the simple phrases of such a hero, here is not only victory and courage, but love sublimer and superior.'

The youngster from Newcastle's rough and ready quayside, the grammar school pupil, the cabin boy that rose to the second highest rank in the Royal Navy would have dismissed this description of himself; Cuthbert Collingwood would not have been comfortable with such a public statement of his abilities. But the private Tynesider would have taken quiet satisfaction that his life of service to his country had been recognised as worthy and honourable.

A posthumous portait

THE COLLINGWOOD
INHERITANCE

If you seek his monument, look round[2]

On the death of their mother, the Collingwood daughters, Sarah and Mary Patience, erected a cenotaph at their own expense inside St Nicholas' Cathedral, Newcastle. The inscription was to both their parents and it stands in an imposing position inside the entrance. A tribute at the time of the unveiling, declared:

> 'He has the right to be considered the noblest of Englishmen that ever trod a quarterdeck. He was a typical north countryman, never duly elated at success or depressed by failure, caring little for popular applause, quiet and retiring in his ways, anxious only to serve his country to the best of his ability.'

The monument is a bust of Collingwood on a square pedestal with full drapery behind in a typically decorative, heroic representation of the period. It might not have been to the modest taste of Cuthbert but he would have appreciated the family gesture. The memorial's inscription summarises Collingwood's career and an extract reiterates the City of Newcastle's pride at the achievements of her most famous son:

St. Nicholas' Cathedral and castle keep 1980

> 'In the memorable battle of Trafalgar he led the British squadrons into action and pressing forward with his single ship into the midst of the combined fleets of France and Spain. On that day after the death of his illustrious commander and friend Lord Nelson he completed the most decisive and glorious victory that is recorded in the naval annuls of the world.'

Twenty-eight years after Collingwood's death it was proposed that a commemorative monument should be erected and permission was given by Parliament. The memorial would be paid for by public subscriptions and an early letter to the press welcomed the tribute and suggested that 'a colossal pillar, with or without a statue, should be situated on the western or higher part of the Town Moor' - open land on the outskirts of the city. This very year, 1838, was the year that the 41-metre tall Earl Grey monument was erected in Newcastle as part of the burgeoning Grainger Town development - his Lordship had been a humane Prime Minister and also had a blend of tea

Collingwood Street, 2004

named after him. Collingwood Street had already been laid out with three-storey red-bricked houses with shop fronts (none of which have survived) and it was felt that the Vice-Admiral ought to have a similar memorial to compliment the Earl's column at the top of Grey Street. The coming of the railways and John Dobson's plans for the Newcastle Central Station restricted the land space to the west of the city so the decision to find a suitable site languished for many months in the committee rooms of Mansion House. The dignitaries might have pondered indefinitely but it was the coal-owner Matthew White Ridley, Vice-Chairman of the Collingwood Memorial Committee, who got things moving. Mr J G Lough, the local sculptor, had been commissioned to produce a huge seven metre stone statue, which came in thirteen pieces and weighed thirty tons. The figure [see back cover] was described as having a classical appearance:

'It is partly clothed in a boat cloak that is made to hang with grace and dignity. The likeness to Lord Collingwood is correct, the impression is firm, noble and decisive, but not obstinate, and dignified without asperity. The whole is pure, grand and simple.'

Newcastle-upon-Tyne was Collingwood's birthplace but many felt that the monument deserved a coastal location. An editorial in the *Port of Tyne* publication dated November 1840 stated:

'Reasons for putting up the tribute in a spot overlooking the ocean rather than in the city, can be summed up:

-A marine location, with cliffs and shores where our hero spent his happiest hours.

-Family choice. Lord Collingwood's family remain here at Chirton. It is also a matter of taste to be overlooking the sublime element where deeds of glory were achieved, rather than coop it up around the smoky streets, and vulgar, everyday life of the population of a large commercial town, where the passer-by is bustling after his worldly affairs. Surely the bold headlands of Tynemouth are preferable.'

The persuasive words of the editor did not convince all of the city dignitaries for many of them withdrew their donations when Tynemouth was agreed upon. Consequently, the proposed column would be reduced in size. The *Port of Tyne*, however, continued to promote the coastal site and told its readership:

'Mr John Davidson, foreman at Messers Pow and Fawcus's chain and anchor manufactory, Reed Street, North Shields, collected the very handsome sum of £5-8s-9d as the contribution of the men employed in the said manufactory towards the Collingwood monument - an act which is highly honourable to the horny-handed and noble-minded fellows, and an example we should rejoice to see followed by others of the townsmen.'

By May 1841, Matthew Ridley must have been relieved that a decision had finally been reached; at last the great man would be raised in stature at the most easterly point along the Northumberland coastline. Lough's effigy would gaze out to sea within the confines of the ancient priory churchyard; it would be 'a fitting memorial to a great Christian leader, and act as a noble beacon to seafarers.' Ridley declared that this would be the favoured site and added 'providing no objections are made by the relatives of any deceased person who may be interred within the space required.'

The priory grounds also happened to be within the parish church of St Mary's and yes, there was an objection. A belligerent letter-writer to the local newspaper insisted that the Collingwood Memorial committee had no right to 'interfere with the graves of deceased parishioners in consecrated ground.' The anonymous protester was determined that Ridley and his colleagues should be resisted:

'Nothing short of an Act of Parliament passed for the purpose, can authorise the monument's erection in the burial ground at Tynemouth.'

A few weeks later the committee received an emphatic response from the clergy:

'I Christopher Reed, Vicar of Tynemouth, in consequence of several of the parishioners having represented to me that the erecting of a memorial to the late Lord Collingwood on the south-east corner of the burial ground, many of the graves of their relatives would be interfered with, and their feelings hurt. Therefore I refuse permission to it being placed on that spot.'

The vicar, at a stroke, had set back the progress once more. What next? The discussions began again and a site was suggested on the level ground between the Prior's Haven beach and the Spanish battery - now a car park. The battery had been constructed at the time of Henry the Eighth and guns were positioned there to protect the mouth of the River Tyne. It was argued that this would be a vulnerable spot for the statue because the column would act as a marker for

The Tynemouth headland, 2004

enemy gun-sights at sea. In defence of the site the Collingwood supporters maintained that in the heat of action, with guns blazing, that is exactly where the Vice-Admiral would have wanted to be positioned.

Whilst the debate was continuing, a 45-metre fluted, Corinthian column was being erected in the newly created Trafalgar Square in central London and in 1843 a 5-metre stone statue of Lord Nelson was placed on the top. Coincidentally, around this time, the French, in a display of post-Bonaparte nostalgia, constructed their own Napoleon column at Boulogne [3 metres taller than Nelson's column] to commemorate the base camp where the Emperor had amassed his 115,000 invasion force. This outbreak of heroic monuments seemed to galvanise the Collingwood committee and they turned to the Duke of Northumberland to help them break the deadlock. The Duke's father had kept up a correspondence with Cuthbert after Trafalgar so he generously donated the present land, 200 metres inland of the Spanish battery. The position, overlooking the Black Middens - a notorious area for shipwrecks - seemed to satisfy all parties, and the Duke even kick-started the dwindling public subscriptions by donating £500. The cash boost allowed local architect John Dobson to build his impressive pedestal with its stone steps which visitors could walk around and admire not just the column, but also the spectacular coastal and river views. It was finally constructed in 1845 - seven years after the inception - and two years later the final touch was added with the placement of four thirty-two pound cannons from the *Royal Sovereign* which were the first English guns to be fired in the great battle of Trafalgar.

At the opening ceremony the Newcastle Journal editorial paid tribute to Collingwood for his 'matchless skill and courage as a statesman and warrior.' With more than a hint of hyperbole the editor wrote:

'Let Cuthbert Collingwood's monument, towering to the skies, lift its tall head from the mouth of her noble river like another Colossus at the entrance of Rhodes.'

And what of the Collingwood family after the Vice-Admiral's death? In the edition of The Times dated 22nd November 1819 there was an announcement of the death of 'the Right Hon. Lady Collingwood at Tynemouth on the 17th inst.' Sarah senior, aged 57, had died nine-and-a-half years after her husband and it was reported that she would be 'universally lamented.' In their mother's will, which showed her address as 'York Place in the county of Middlesex', the daughters were given equal shares of the family fortune.

On the 30th May 1816, two days after her 26th birthday, Cuthbert's daughter, Sarah, married a barrister, George Lewis Newnham. Mr Newnham would shortly add Collingwood to his surname and he would publish, with his own personal observations, selected letters from his father-in-law's correspondence. This 'life' of the Commander-in-Chief ran into five editions (last reprint 1837) and proved to be a Georgian best-seller. The family had been disappointed that Lord Collingwood's peerage had not been passed on through his daughters but in an attempt to rectify the omission of royal patronage George Lewis Newnham dedicated his book to King George IV and felt sure this gesture would be worth a barony at the very least. The book caught the imagination of the public, but evidently did not excite king, for Sarah's husband was destined to remain G L Newnham Collingwood esquire. Cuthbert's correspondence, particularly the letters to his daughters, where he offers his opinions on their personal morality, temperament and education, went down very well with a readership that was preparing for the coronation of a young and impressionable Queen Victoria.

Mary Patience was described by her father as a 'spirited dame' and for a while she refused to conform to the family dictates. She was betrothed to her father's secretary, Mr W R Cosway, but Collingwood's younger brother, Uncle John, persuaded her to break off the engagement. He, and the family, felt that the son of a baker was not a appropriate match for the daughter of a peer of the realm. In 1817, she found a suitable suitor and at the age of twenty-four, married Mr Anthony Denny with the family's blessing. Mary Patience would bring children into the world but unluckily she did not inherit the Collingwood longevity gene and died two days after her thirtieth birthday.

Cuthbert's 'little Sall' as he called his daughter Sarah, was the last to go. The Newcastle Journal dated November 29th 1851 reported her death:

At Dover on the 25th instant in the 59th year of her age after a few days' illness the Honourable Sarah Newnham Collingwood, eldest daughter of the late Admiral Cuthbert Lord Collingwood of Chirton, Northumberland and granddaughter of the late John Erasmus Blackett Esquire an Alderman of Newcastle Upon Tyne and wife of the late George Lewis Newnham Collingwood Esquire of Hawkhurst Kent.

The silver kettle

Before her death, Sarah had become a little eccentric. She had outlived her husband by several years and now, a lonely widow in the south of England, Sarah began distributing many of her father's treasures to favourite maids and casual acquaintances. A inscribed silver kettle presented to Cuthbert Collingwood by the City of Newcastle after Trafalgar, valued at £150 guineas [£16,000 = 2004] was given to her young servant as a wedding present. It was retrieved years later and purchased by the Laing Art Gallery in Newcastle. Sarah gave birth to two daughters but neither, as they phrased it in the 19th century, 'gave issue'.

On the death of Lord Collingwood, the Chirton Estate passed into the hands of the next male in line, Uncle John. John married late in life; he was in his sixties and it was after the death of his famous, elder brother. His demise was in 1840 and it was Edward John, his eldest son, who inherited the land and property. On Edward's death (1876) the estate was qacquired by Mr William Hedley which ended the 150-year Collingwood residency. At the time of writing, a petrol filling station is on the site of the colliery and a boarded-up, due-for-demolition public house, named 'The Collingwood' is the last surviving reminder of the family connection.

Collingwood's name lives on in streets and thoroughfares and on public buildings. The Royal Grammar School continue to remember their illustrious pupil each year on Trafalgar Day when a bowl of flowers is placed beneath his portrait. Sadly his name has not always been respected. In Tynemouth village, Cuthbert's memory was kept alive in the 'Royal Sovereign' public house affectionately known for many years as the 'Sov'. Recently the Collingwood connection was severed when the brewers changed the name, inexplicably, to 'The Furry Pear'.

The Tynesider's fame, however, spread beyond these shores and reached a Canadian bay in Ontario that was known as Hen and Chickens Harbour. In 1854 the settlers in the area renamed their township Collingwood to honour the British hero and with the coming of the railroad the community soon became an established centre for shipping and shipbuilding. Today Collingwood is a thriving town and ski resort with a resident population of 13,500 and they remain proud of their association with the Northumbrian Admiral.

The monument

The thirty-two ships that Collingwood served in or commanded:

HMS *Shannon* 1760 (under Braithwaite) age 12
HMS *Gibraltar*, HMS *Liverpool*, HMS *Lennox*, HMS *Portland*, HMS *Preston*,
HMS *Lively*, HMS *Somerset*, HMS *Hornet*, HMS *Lowestoffe*, HMS *Bristol*,
HMS *Badger* [commander] 1779, HMS *Hinchinbroke* [Post Captain] 1780,
HMS *Pelican* 1781, HMS *Samson* 1783, HMS *Mediator* 1783, HMS *Mermaid* 1790,
HMS *Prince* [flag captain] 1793, HMS *Barfleur* 1794, HMS *Hector* 1794,
HMS *Excellent* 1797, HMS *Triumph* 1799, HMS *Barfleur* 1800, HMS *Diamond* 1803,
HMS *Venerable* 1803, HMS *Minotaur* 1803, HMS *Culloden* 1803,
HMS *Dreadnought* 1804, HMS *Royal Sovereign* [Rear-Admiral] 1805,
HMS *Euryalus* 1805, HMS *Ocean* [Vice-Admiral] 1807, HMS V*ille de Paris* 1809.

[1] The chapter quotes are taken from the song 'Heart of Oak' written by the famous actor David Garrick in 1759 to celebrate the Royal Navy's 'Year of Victories'.
[2] Inscription in St. Paul's Cathedral written by the son of Sir Christopher Wren.
Pictures on pages 18, 30 and 93 by kind permission of the Collingwood family.

Bibliography

The Life and letters of Vice-Admiral Lord Collingwood by Oliver Warner.
Oxford University Press 1968
Admiral Lord Collingwood by Boris Klukvin. Oriel Press 1972
Correspondence of Vice-Admiral Lord Collingwood. Memoirs of his Life
                       by G L Newnham Collingwood. James Ridgeway 1837
The Royal Grammar School by Mains and Tuck. Oriel Press 1986
Nelson's Battles by Oliver Warner. David and Charles Press 1971
Nelson and his World by Tom Pocock. Thames and Hudson 1968
Nelson by David Walder. Hamish Hamilton 1978
Nelson by Oliver Warner. Weidenfeld and Nicolson 1975
The Wooden Fighting Ship by E.H.H. Archibald. Blandford Press 1972
Nelson: The essential Hero by Ernie Bradford. Macmillan 1977
Nelson by Roy Hattersley. Weidenfeld and Nicolson 1974
Men Twixt Tide and Tweed by Richard Welford. 1894
Horatio Nelson by Tom Pocock. The Bodley Head 1987
Nelson by Carola Oman. Hodder and Stoughton 1967
Nelson. A personal History by Christopher Hibbert. Viking 1994